CONGREGATION
SHAAREY ZEDEK
5622-5742   1861-1981

CONGREGATION SHAAREY ZEDEK

5622-5742   1861-1981

by Eli Grad and Bette Roth

דּוֹר לְדוֹר יְשַׁבַּח מַעֲשֶׂיךָ וּגְבוּרֹתֶיךָ יַגִּידוּ׃

Thy works shall be praised from generation to generation

Congregation Shaarey Zedek   Southfield, Michigan   1982

Compiled and edited by Carol Altman Bromberg.
Designed by Richard Kinney and Mary Primeau.

Produced for Congregation Shaarey Zedek by Wayne
State University Press, Detroit, Michigan, 48202.

Library of Congress Cataloging in Publication Data

Grad, Eli.
   Congregation Shaarey Zedek, 5622-5742,
1861-1981.

   Includes bibliographical references.
   1. Congregation Shaarey Zedek (Southfield,
Mich.) — History. 2. Jews — Michigan — Detroit —
History. 3. Jews — Michigan — Southfield —
History. I. Roth, Bette. II. Congregation
Shaarey Zedek (Southfield, Mich.). III. Title.
BM225.S682C664 296.8'342'0977434   82-4865
ISBN 0-8143-1713-8   AACR2

The years granted to Moses were 120; at his death, the Bible tells us that "His eyes were undimmed and his vigor unabated." Hence, the customary felicitation in our tradition on a birthday or anniversary: *ad meah v'esrim*, which means "until 120," the years of vigor granted to Moses. But what can be said when one has fortunately reached the 120th anniversary? For this, too, Jewish tradition has an appropriate blessing: *ken yirbu* — "May the years, and the blessings, and the joys multiply."

Rabbi Irwin Groner

CONTENTS

"ועשו לי מקדש ושכנתי בתוכם"

"And establish for Me a sanctuary
and I will dwell in their midst."

EXODUS 25:8

The United Synagogue of America

in convention assembled takes note of those special
synagogues in our midst that are 120 years old
and have continued to this day to serve the
American Jewish community.
We cite with great pride

Congregation Shaarey Zedek
Southfield, Michigan

which was established 120 years ago and helped to
lay the foundation for a flourishing
Jewish community.

This congregation with its inspired leadership made
possible the establishment of other synagogues and
temples and educational institutions that are the
keystones of our religious life.

We offer our prayers for God's continued blessings
upon the leadership and the members of this sacred
congregation. May they continue to walk stead-
fastly in the ways of our tradition and glorify
the name of God in our midst.

November 18, 1981
22 Heshvan, 5742

Simon Schwartz
President

Benjamin Z. Kreitman
Executive Vice President

Every celebration — it has often been observed — is in large measure an affirmation. This is true of our holidays and festivals, which, each in its season, remind us of ideas and values important to our tradition. Just so, the celebration of the birthday of a synagogue is an affirmation of our identification with the values which the synagogue embodies.

The celebration of the one hundred twentieth anniversary of Shaarey Zedek surpasses the normal joy for such an occasion because this milestone proclaims the centrality of one of the great synagogues of our people in the life of its community. Shaarey Zedek today, as throughout its long history, reflects a genuine vitality. Like the great institutions of old, it has transcended the change, and even the decline, of its physical surroundings, translating itself again and again into the setting and idiom of its time and place.

Shaarey Zedek is a significant mirror of the history of the American Jewish community, reflecting above all its capacity for an effective religious response to its environment. By moving with its congregation physically from one location to another, and, indeed, by blazing the trail in each change of location, this synagogue has demonstrated its determination to shape its constituency spiritually. It has become an umbilical cord, tying the Jewish legacy to a Jewish future sustained by classical visions. The volume before us is a record both of the history of Shaarey Zedek and of the community which the congregation has shaped and inspired. It tells the story in a way that makes it a document which will be treasured by historians of American Jewry. It is a lively record that reveals the sources of the synagogue's continuing vitality.

Shaarey Zedek has attained the impressive age of 120. The years have not always sat easily on the congregation. It survived the trauma of seeing its beloved rabbi, Morris Adler, shot down literally before its eyes in front of the open Ark. It has overcome severe financial problems. Always, its indomitable spirit has triumphed over tragedy and adversity.

One demonstration of its powerful life force was the succession of Rabbi Groner to this pulpit, after the year of mourning for Rabbi Adler. Another is the continued presence of Goldie Adler and her participation in every aspect of synagogue life. In the years since 1966, these two indomitable people have set an example of how a living memorial is created, and the congregation has followed their leadership. Their fallen leader was never forgotten, but the growth of the congregation, its spiritual health and strength, were always the primary consideration.

It is noteworthy that, in its early years, the congregation anteceded the great waves of Jewish immigration. Shaarey Zedek and its leaders had ample time to experience the loneliness of Jews on the American frontier. But when the great numbers began to arrive a century ago, the congregation was in the forefront of the

9

institutions guiding Jews in their adjustment to their new environment. Its importance has been that its membership has always felt the impact and outreach of its spiritual leadership to the community at large.

In those early days there was no Jewish Theological Seminary to guide and inspire those who sought an adaptation of Judaism that would remain within the bounds of tradition. For a quarter of a century or more, the congregation and its spiritual leaders had to struggle on their own with problems of language, of ritual, and of custom. When the Seminary was founded in 1886, it linked the congregation to the larger community. By that time, Shaarey Zedek was one of the handful of congregations which in retrospect we would identify as conservative.

It is of significance to note that in this sense there were conservative congregations before there was a movement identified as Conservative Judaism, or a Seminary to prepare leaders for it. Among other things, this fact is evidence of the authenticity of our movement and of its central institutions. While Conservative Judaism has, over the years, become increasingly able to articulate its position and to explain how it attempts to interpret Jewish tradition in its application to life in America, it has never been a didactic movement, imposing a set of norms upon affiliated congregations. Indeed, our movement reflects the true nature of religious development, with changes often beginning at the grass roots level and finally winning acceptance and theological rationale from the theoreticians and academicians. Thus it was in a sense congregations like Shaarey Zedek which had a profound impact on the shape and content of the Seminary's message. Once the Seminary came into being, the relationship became symbiotic, with each partner contributing its special strengths. As you celebrate your 120th anniversary, and we approach our centennial, we are each able to perceive our dependence upon the other, and to see our relationship, and the movement which rests on it, as indispensable to the vitality of Judaism in America.

In conclusion, I must take this opportunity to congratulate the congregation and its leadership on the wisdom you have shown in choosing to prepare and publish this volume. There could be no better way of observing so significant an anniversary in your institutional life than by authorizing this careful chronicle of your past.

On this foundation, and with the continuing wise guidance of your rabbi and lay leadership, the congregation can embark upon its second 120 years, with every confidence that it will continue to grow from strength to strength.

Gerson D. Cohen
Chancellor,
The Jewish Theological Seminary of America

ACKNOWLEDGMENTS

Because this book is the story of a congregation of people, acknowledgment rightfully must first be made to their several generations. Although the fact is obvious, it is no less necessary to note that without their dedicated participation over the past one hundred and twenty years there could be no history of the Shaarey Zedek synagogue. To Eli Grad and Bette Roth was given the task of gathering together the history of the congregation; Eli Grad assumed responsibility for the narrative up to 1961, and Bette Roth continued the story to the present. This volume has been extracted from their carefully prepared texts.

Rabbi Irwin Groner, with characteristic wisdom and energy, responded to the many queries that arose along the way; and his sense of perspective and good humor made the way pleasant. Judith Cantor enthusiastically accepted the challenge to locate documents, while Charlotte Shapiro placed her skills and excellent memory at the disposal of the project. Goldie Adler, an integral part of the modern Shaarey Zedek, helped breathe life into cold facts.

Special mention must be accorded to Virginia Fried, Marjorie Saulson, Harriet Siden, Nettie Weinberg, Oscar Kramer, and Mr. and Mrs. Aid Kushner for their many services. The staunch support of Walter L. Field, Philip Slomovitz, and Allen Warsen greatly facilitated the task of composing a balanced history. Much of the background material has been drawn from the archives of Temple Beth El, and, hence, part of this volume belongs to the legacy left by Irving I. Katz; to his widow Gail Katz gratitude is extended.

Harvey L. Weisberg, president of the congregation, and past president Harold Berry have provided the practical encouragement, and Irwin T. Holtzman the determination of the true bibliophile, necessary to transform an idea into a book.

Much of this history has been won from scattered documents, but a large part has also been winnowed from memory, from family albums and scrapbooks. A list of those who have provided such information, who have volunteered anecdotes and treasured memories in interviews, would repeat most of the names of the families on the membership list of Congregation Shaarey Zedek. The photographs have come from many sources; only a few can be credited to specific photographic services. Those known and deserving of mention are: the Detroit newspapers (the *Times, News,* and *Free Press,*) the White House, The Detroit Institute of Arts, Albert Kahn Assocs., Press Picture Service, O. R. Forster Co., Manning Bros., Heinz Photo, Blair Studio, Paramount Photo, Joseph P. Messana, Zalman Cohen, Henry L. Lerman, Marvin Lehrman, Bernard H. Winer, Benyas-Kaufman, Percival Goodman, Balthazar Korab, Jules Fayne Studio, Leo Knight, and Associated Food Dealers. Some illustrations have been reproduced from I. I. Katz, *The Jewish Soldier from Michigan in the Civil War*, I. I. Katz, *The Beth El Story*, and S. Farmer, *History of Detroit and Wayne County and Early Michigan*.

It is inevitable that the careful eye will discover in the pages that follow an error of omission, a wrong identification, a misspelled name, a questionable date; certainly a much longer volume could have been written with many more people and events important to the life of the synagogue noted and expanded upon. But if these pages communicate a feeling of the vitality and historical purpose of the synagogue — that coming together of many families in one American community in common purpose and dedication — it is a task well done.

The Editor
May, 1982

"Let them make Me a sanctuary, that I may dwell among them." Ever since that ancient command was given to the children of Israel in the wilderness in the days of Moses, they have erected sanctuaries consecrated to the service of God. With the destruction of the ancient Temple in Jerusalem in the year 70 C.E., synagogues became the spiritual citadels of the Jewish people, who shared a heritage and a hope in all the lands of their settlement.

Moved by that spirit, a group of seventeen men banded together to form a Jewish congregation known as Shaarey Zedek in Detroit, Michigan, in 1861. With great personal devotion, they established a House of God to declare their faith in their ancestral religion. The synagogue was the affirmation of their will to endure as a religious fellowship, the embodiment of their loyalty to the Almighty, to Torah, and to Israel.

We celebrate the 120th year of Congregation Shaarey Zedek with a publication of its history. Shaarey Zedek's record is a distinguished one, marking its role in the development of Conservative Judaism in Detroit and in America and the part its leaders have played in creating, nurturing, and guiding the institutions of the Detroit Jewish community. It is not unseemly that this congregation reviews its past and confers honor upon its founders and leaders with proper and justifiable pride.

This work has relevance beyond the confines of this congregation, for the portrait of Shaarey Zedek reveals the encounter of traditional Judaism and a free society. Shaarey Zedek's growth and development were made possible by the opportunities and the congenial environment which America offered to Jews who came here from an Old World of cruelty and oppression to build a new life.

Those who arrived in Detroit, as in the other cities of America, carried in their hearts the fullness of a precious heritage — the faith of Abraham, the law of Moses, the vision of the prophets, the wisdom of the sages, the unfailing hope of the people of Israel. Although they had left the ghetto or the shtetl, they affirmed their determination to preserve for themselves and their children the vitality of the Jewish tradition through their loyalty and devotion to their synagogue. In responding to the challenge of industrial growth and social change, they adapted the synagogue to meet the changing needs of the American Jew, creating new forms of religious expression in which traditional Jewish values and practices were expressed in the American idiom. Thus, the history of Shaarey Zedek provides a vivid and significant commentary on both the strength of Jewish commitment and the spirit of America.

These six score years, years of world wars and global upheavals, have brought changes which have transformed the character of American and world Jewry: the mass immigration of Jews from Eastern Europe to the New World; the growth and development of the American Jewish community; the Holocaust and the destruction of European Jewry; the continuing travail of Israel in her quest for security and peace; and the struggle of Soviet Jewry for freedom. The American Jewish community has responded to the challenges of its historic responsibility. As one examines the annals of Shaarey Zedek, one notes the streams of influence and support that flowed from this congregation to the centers of Jewish life everywhere.

We live on the frontier of a constantly changing world, facing problems and challenges that seem unprecedented. Assimilation with American culture has led to a weakening of Jewish ideals and standards to which former generations were loyal; American Jews have paid a high price for integration in a free society. The decline in the strength of the family has serious consequences for a way of life preserved by the transmission of tradition from one generation to the next. In a secular world, religious values are often regarded with skepticism. We suffer from depersonalization and alienation and struggle with breaks and gashes in our social fabric.

In response to these concerns, Shaarey Zedek has developed programs which personalize the synagogue and generate a sense of community. Distinguished scholars enlarge our vision and broaden our understanding. Religious education develops new curricula and methodologies to engage the mind and heart of the young. Increased emphasis is placed on strengthening the Jewish family, as the center of the transmission for Jewish values.

But, as we face the future, we ask whether this congregation will be equal to the tasks that lie ahead. As a people, we have withstood persecution and exclusion. Can we remain Jews in this land with its climate of acceptance and tolerance? In a world beset by dislocation and turbulence, will the synagogue continue to provide a sense of the sacred and enduring meaning of human existence?

A Jew was defined by Yehuda Ha-Levi, the distinguished poet and philosopher of the Golden Age, as a "prisoner of hope." Because we are prisoners of hope, we believe that the heritage of 120 years will be renewed in the generation of the future. The American synagogue has conveyed the meaning of Jewish existence to the largest Jewish community that has ever lived in a free society. We believe that Shaarey Zedek can preserve the best of our past as it inspires its sons and daughters to Jewish idealism and faithfulness.

In 1907, Dr. Israel Friedlander, an East European professor at The Jewish Theological Seminary of America, offered his fellow Americans a vision: "We perceive a community great in numbers, mighty in power; actively participating in civic, social and economic progress of the country, yet deeply rooted in the soil of Judaism, clinging to its past, working for its future, true to its traditions, faithful to its aspirations, attached to the land of their fathers as the cradle and resting place of the Jewish spirit; . . . a sharply marked community, distinct and distinguished, trusted for its loyalty, respected for its dignity, esteemed for its tradition, valued for its aspiration. . . ."

If, in the midst of freedom and security, Jews can reaffirm their witness to God's presence and His truth, this modern vision and prophecy may yet come true. Let the record of Congregation Shaarey Zedek fortify in us the strength and the determination to fulfill this task for the decades ahead.

Rabbi Irwin Groner

I. The Early Years
1850-1921

Detroit of 1850 was a small town, its population of twenty-one thousand concentrated near the waterfront. The city extended from Dequindre Street on the east to what is now Eighth Street on the west. There were a few scattered houses as far north as Grand Circus Park, beyond which there were farms. The most popular residential streets were Woodbridge, Jefferson, Congress, Larned, and Fort.

Homes were lit with tallow candles or lamps that burned lard or whale oil. The first derby hats had appeared on Detroit's streets, and women wore long, full skirts with many flounces over hoops or starched petticoats. High-heeled buttoned shoes and small hats and bonnets trimmed with plumes completed the costume. Those who dared caused considerable public commotion by appearing in bloomer dresses: three-quarter-length skirts over Turkish trousers.

Detroiters shared the indignation of many of their fellow Americans over the plight of the black slaves. Because it was so close to Canada, Detroit had become a major depot in the underground railway which smuggled runaway slaves into Canada. Brought to the city disguised as merchandise, the fugitives would be hidden in the livery stable owned by Seymour Finney on the corner of Griswold and State. There, they waited until it was dark, when they could safely cross the river into Canada. Ironically, the slave-masters who were hunting these slaves stayed in the hotel owned by Seymour Finney at Woodward and Gratiot.

Despite substantial increases in the population of Detroit throughout the 1840s, the number of Jews in early 1850 was small. The city directory of 1850 lists A. Amberg & Company, merchant tailors; S. & H. Bendit & Company, dry goods; Solomon Cohen, peddler; S. Freedman & Brothers, dry goods dealers; Alexander Grunwald, clothing store; Joseph Grunwald; the firm of Silberman & Hersch, cigar manufacturers; and Leopold Pappenkeimer, fancy store.

During the course of the year, the Jewish population of Detroit rose to approximately sixty. (The total Jewish population of the United States was about fifty thousand.) Among the Jews who settled in Detroit in 1850 were Isaac and Sarah Cozens, a German-Jewish couple who arrived from New York and took up residence in a house near the corner of Congress and St. Antoine streets.

Before long, the number of Jews who wanted to worship together reached a minyan, and the first Jewish religious service, conducted by Marcus Cohen, took place at the Cozens' home. On September 22, 1850, twelve German Jews organized the Beth El Society at a meeting held at the Cozens' home. This was the first Jewish congregation in Michigan. The new congregation, Orthodox in its ritual and observances, engaged Rabbi Samuel Marcus of New York as its first rabbi at an annual salary of two hundred dollars, not an insignificant amount when one bears in mind that the finest seven-course dinner in town cost twenty-five cents. Rabbi Marcus also

The first Jewish services in Detroit were held at the home of Isaac and Sarah Cozens, near Congress and St. Antoine streets.

Marcus Cohen served as lay rabbi of Beth El before the congregation hired its first ordained rabbi.

19

Rabbi Liebman Adler, rabbi of Beth El from 1854-1861.

acted as cantor, shochet, mohel, and teacher in the Hebrew-English day school in which the congregation's children received both their secular and religious education. (The United States did not have a system of free public education at this time; hence, every group established, as best it could, its own form of private instruction.)

On January 1, 1851, the congregation purchased half an acre of land on Champlain (now Lafayette Street) to use as a cemetery for one hundred fifty dollars. The Beth El Society was legally incorporated on April 21, 1851. The articles of incorporation provided for an Orthodox mode of worship: "If the Congregation secures a Synagogue or other building for Divine Services, such Services shall be held according to Minhag Ashkenaz [German ritual] and not be changed as long as the Congregation exists under the name of Bet El." A Chevra Bikur Cholim, a society for the relief of the sick, was organized with Charles E. Bresler as its president. After a year of meeting in private homes, the congregation rented a room above Silberman and Hersch's store at 172 Jefferson Avenue to be used as a place of worship.

Beth El lost its first rabbi in the summer of 1854. Among the victims of a cholera epidemic which ravaged Detroit for three months was Rabbi Samuel Marcus. The congregation turned to Dr. Isaac Mayer Wise of Cincinnati, the founder of American Reform Judaism, for advice in the selection of a new rabbi. On his recommendation, they hired Dr. Liebman Adler, who had just arrived from Germany. His annual salary was three hundred sixty dollars, and his duties included that of preacher (in German), cantor, teacher, shochet, and mohel.

During this period in American Jewish history, a struggle had begun between advocates of tradition and those who were in favor of reform. Both causes were supported by outstanding Jewish leaders dedicated to a vibrant, meaningful Judaism. Rabbi Isaac Leeser of Philadelphia was a staunch traditionalist who sought to preserve long-revered doctrines and practices of Judaism by introducing English-language sermons, promoting Jewish education, and strengthening ties to Jewish culture. The cause of reform was championed by Rabbi Wise, who composed impassioned sermons and articles in favor of a less strict interpretation of the observance of Judaism. For a time the forces of traditionalism and reform strove to maintain harmony through cooperation and compromise. In 1848-49, Rabbis Leeser and Wise issued a joint call to congregational leaders throughout the country in an effort to convoke a national meeting, but only eight synagogues responded.

In 1855 they tried a different approach: a rabbinical conference. In October of that year, rabbis representing both the traditionalist and reform points of view convened in Cleveland at the first ecclesiastical gathering of American Jewry. Among them was Rabbi Liebman Adler of Beth El. The conference began in the spirit of harmony, with both sides willing to compromise on certain theological issues for the sake of unity. But during the conference, Rabbi Leeser had to leave for Philadelphia, and the traditionalists were left without their spokesman. The reformers decided that they had compromised enough and passed some resolutions which encouraged Rabbi Adler to promote reform at Beth El, but completely alienated the Orthodox camp.

By 1855 the congregation had twenty-five members, and one thousand dollars was raised for the purchase of a site for a synagogue. Under the leadership of Rabbi Adler, reform made rapid inroads into the practices of the congregation. However, this was not acceptable to many members; the congregation appears to have been evenly divided among those who believed in reform and those who maintained that changes in ritual would endanger the structure of Judaism.

In 1856 a new constitution and by-laws were adopted containing some elements of reform, and the schism which was to result in the organization of a new congregation just five years later was under way. The new constitution provided that

> the Congregation shall, in all its religious institutions, pay due attention to the progress of the age, and maintain the respect due to customs or laws handed down to us by our pious fathers. In cases of innovation, this Congregation shall attempt to remain in unity with the majority, at least, of the American Congregations, and shall always attempt to produce uniformity in the American Synagogue.

The new by-laws provided for the removal of certain portions from the service: all Selichos (penitential prayers), except on the Yamim Noraim, and most Kinos (lamentations) for the ninth day of Av were among the many prayers which were abolished.

Just one year later, Rabbi Leeser visited Beth El. After observing its services and meeting its members, he wrote in *The Occident:*

> We also learned that some reforms have been introduced into the worship, such as reading the Haphtorah in a German translation, and having some prayers in the same language in place of the Yakum Purkan; but we also perceived that the whole people were not satisfied with what had been done and nearly all would resist any radical and farther changes. We trust that for the sake of the public peace, no more alterations will be attempted; for it is one thing to have order, but quite another to force measures on a part of the community which would necessarily provoke resistance.

Rabbi Wise visited Beth El three times between 1856 and 1861 to lend his support to Rabbi Adler's efforts to introduce innovations.

There was still no synagogue structure in 1859, and Rabbi Adler submitted his resignation. He was persuaded to stay with the congregation, but repeatedly urged the members to build a synagogue. Finally a building association was formed with Edward Kanter as its president. In the meantime, a hall was rented over John C.

The Rev. L. Adler is the popular minister of this [Beth El] congregation. He attempted successfully to improve divine services by his lectures, exegetic expositions of the biblical sections read every Sabbath, and by omitting from the liturgy such prayers as belong to bygone ages. Three times a week Mr. A. gives instruction to the young in the religion of our fathers. In consequence of Mr. A.'s being Shochet and Mohel he cannot attend as fully as he desires to the functions of a teacher. Our brethren in Detroit have no Synagogue of their own and no expectation to get one very soon. There is not that enterprise and energy in congregational affairs among our brethren of Detroit as among the rest of our Western congregations. They need a synagogue, a school, a benevolent society, and they could have all these with but little exertion on the part of the leading members. Several of them told us they would contribute several hundred dollars toward the building of a new synagogue; this is the case especially with Messrs. Breslauer, Sykes and others, if the matter would be agitated.

The Israelite, *August 26, 1859*

Rivard Street synagogue; Beth El's first building, purchased in 1861.

The Hebrew Synagogue was dedicated yesterday. It is a neat substantial building, the inside arrangement being, with the exception of the holy arch, so near like our churches, that no description of it need be given.

At 3 o'clock P.M. the ceremonies commenced with a Hebrew song by the choir accompanied by a melodeon, during which Rev. Mr. Lasar, Mr. S. Freedman and Mr. Schloss carried the sacred scrolls of the law in procession through the Synagogue, preceded by six girls dressed in white, carrying burning white tapers.

The Detroit Tribune and Advertiser,
August, 1861

Scherer's drugstore at 39 Michigan Grand Avenue, between Bates and Randolph, at an annual rental of one hundred forty dollars.

The traditionalists among the members of Beth El continued to challenge reform at every opportunity. The meeting of March 4, 1860, was the scene of bitterness and name-calling when a group of members challenged the legality of the 1856 constitution and by-laws. In the heated debate, the reformers argued that the Orthodox were reactionary fanatics who were holding back the forces of progress and enlightenment; the traditionalists accused the reformers of being radical opportunists who endangered the very future of Judaism. It was only by the slimmest of margins that the constitutional reforms were confirmed.

Efforts to raise funds for a synagogue building continued, and on March 1, 1861, the French Methodist Episcopal Church and adjoining parsonage on Rivard Street between Croghan (now Monroe) and Champlain were purchased for thirty-five hundred dollars. At this time, Rabbi Adler resigned to accept a position at the K.A.M. Temple in Chicago and was succeeded by Rabbi Abraham Laser.

The Rivard Street synagogue was dedicated on Friday afternoon, August 30, 1861. Rabbi Isaac Mayer Wise delivered the dedication sermon. There was a good deal of interest in a well-known oriental traveler who attended the dedication: I.J. Benjamin, who had arrived overland from California on the last lap of a voyage around the world. But the most significant part of the dedication in terms of the future was the musical selections, which featured an organ and a mixed choir, both objectionable to traditionally-oriented members. Upon the move to Rivard Street, the majority of the congregation passed a resolution to establish a choir of men and women to sing at services. Part of the space designated for the women in the gallery was needed for the choir, and some of the women had to occupy seats on the same floor as the men. At the conclusion of Simchas Torah services on September 27, 1861, when these innovations were first introduced, seventeen of the forty members withdrew from Beth El to form the Shaarey Zedek Society. Their first place of worship was the hall above Scherer's drugstore, which had been the original meeting place of the Beth El Society. The seventeen founders of Shaarey Zedek were Isaac and Raphael Epstein, Leopold Fink, Marcus and Jacob Freud, Samuel Fleischman, Hiram Kraushaar, Morris and Ludwig Levy, David Marx, George Morris, Louis Myers, Samuel Newman, Jacob Robinson, Harris Solomon, Isaac Warshauer, and Isaac Wertheimer. Each subscribed one dollar to the treasury. Within a few months, the membership had increased to thirty-six, and Rabbi M. Sapper was engaged as the congregation's spiritual leader.

On June 22, 1862, the society paid four hundred fifty dollars for one and one-half acres of land near the D & M Railroad junction to use as a cemetery, subsequently known as the Smith Street or Beth Olam Cemetery. The articles of incorporation filed with the county clerk on December 12, 1862, were formulated at a meeting held on the fifth of October. Hiram Kraushaar was elected president, and Louis Myers, Samuel Fleischman, Harris Solomon, Leopold Fink, Isaac Warshauer, and Isaac Wertheimer became trustees of the Shaarey Zedek Society.

The period in which seventeen men dedicated to the cause of traditional Judaism formed the Shaarey Zedek Society was that of the Civil War, when the 150 Jewish families of Michigan sent 176 men to the battlefront, an average of more than one soldier per household. In Detroit, tobacco manufacture flourished, as did the stove industry, and the Detroit Bridge and Iron Works was established. The first streetcar line, three miles long, began running on Jefferson Avenue; the cars were pulled by horses at a maximum speed of six miles an hour.

In 1864, Shaarey Zedek had sixty-three members under the leadership of Rabbi Laser Kontrovitch. The women of the congregation had organized an auxiliary to benefit widows and orphans the year before, but there were so few indigent widows and orphans that proceeds from Purim and Simchas Torah balls earmarked for their support produced an excess which was put toward a future orphanage and school. The congregation had also organized a Bikkur Cholim and Chevra Kadisha Society for the relief of the sick and for assistance to bereaved families, with a membership of sixty and a treasury of three hundred dollars. In the event of illness, the society provided a doctor and the necessary medicine and allocated five to six dollars per week for living expenses. Two members of the society were assigned to help each invalid until he had recovered enough to take care of himself.

Now the congregation was ready to purchase a building of its own. For forty-five hundred dollars, they bought an unpretentious frame building on Congress and St. Antoine which had belonged to St. Matthew's Episcopal Church. When the synagogue was dedicated on September 23, 1864, Detroit's mayor, Judge Wilkins, and nearly all of the city aldermen were present. Dr. Isidor Kalisch, rabbi of Beth El, delivered the dedication prayer and a sermon in English.

In 1866, the congregation placed an ad in *The Israelite* for a young man to teach in both Hebrew and German, indicating that Shaarey Zedek provided secular as well as religious education in the days before public school education, but by 1868, Shaarey Zedek children could attend public school. Many parents chose to send their children there, to "Americanize" them, and this, combined with the cost of operating the school, prompted the congregation to limit its educational facilities to religious training.

One of the Simchas Torah Benefit Balls to aid widows and orphans was vividly described in a local paper in 1867:

> Last night a ball was given at Merril Hall for the benefit of the Congregation Scharey Zedeck which was very largely attended by our Jewish

We, the undersigned, George Morris and Samuel Newman, two of the voters nominated by a majority of the voters of the church and congregation hereinafter mentioned as Inspectors at the election of Trustees of the said congregation, do hereby certify: That on the fifth day of October in the year 1862 the male persons of full age belonging to a church in which divine worship is celebrated according to the rite of the Jewish church and not already incorporated, met at the place of public worship heretofor occupied by the said congregation in the City of Detroit in the State of Michigan for the purpose of incorporating themselves and did then and there elect by plurality of votes Hiram Kraushaar, president, Samuel Fleischman, vice president, and said Hiram Kraushaar and said Samuel Fleischman and Louis Myers, Harris Solomon, Leopold Fink, Isaac Warshauer and Isaac Wertheimer as Trustees of the said congregation. And the said persons did then and there also determine by the like plurality of votes that the said Trustees and their successors should be forever hereafter called and known by the name or title of the Trustees of the Shaarey Zedeck.

In testimony whereof we have hereunto set our hands and seals at Detroit, Michigan, this twelfth day of December in the year 1862.

Articles of Incorporation, *1862*

The first building owned by Shaarey Zedek, formerly St. Matthew's Episcopal Church, at Congress and St. Antoine streets; with a seating capacity of five hundred.

Deed dated January 21, 1865, to lot number
four on the south side of Congress Street and
the corner of St. Antoine Street, on the
Antoine Beaubien farm; purchased from
Samuel and Eliza McCloskey by "that Jewish
Religious Society in Corporation in the city of
Detroit known as and called Shaarey Zedeck
of Detroit, Michigan," for the sum of four
thousand dollars.

citizens and proved an admirable success. Dancing was kept up until a late hour this morning and all who participated enjoyed themselves greatly. Those having the affair in charge exerted themselves greatly to please those present. Towards midnight several prominent gentlemen, including Mayor Mills, were introduced by the president of the Congregation, Mr. Kraushaar, to the members of the congregation and were enjoying themselves in a social chit-chat when the pleasantries of the occasion were very much marred by Browse Prentiss who, being called upon, as were the others, to make a few remarks, attempted to turn the affair into a political gathering. That individual commenced a democratic harangue, such as he has been accustomed to making on the stump and the good sense of his hearers prevented his being ejected from the room. They paid little attention to him or his speech and many left the place entirely.

As the congregation grew, its synagogue building became too small, but the sixty-eight members could not afford a new one. In 1876, they appealed to the Jewish community of Detroit for assistance. In a circular the committee of Marcus Freud, Jacob Robinson, S. Keiter, Samuel N. Ginsburg, Manuel Herzberg, and Alexander Tannenholz set forth the congregation's needs:

> The building we now occupy as a Synagogue is a wooden structure, well nigh 30 years old, altogether unworthy of the sacred purposes of worship. Its removal and the substitution of a better and more permanent edifice has become a necessity with us. Our Congregation is limited in members and, while they are taxing themselves to the utmost and are willing to bear burdens in order to accomplish this most desirable object, we still shall be deficient in means.
>
> It is not our intention to indulge in any architectural extravagance or display in these times when money is so scarce, or at least so difficult to reach for purposes of this sort. But the building we propose to erect will, we think, not cost over $12,000.00 and can be put up much more cheaply just now than a year hence. Nevertheless, although costing no more than this sum, we shall, if we succeed in raising the means, present to our worshippers a temple which though of modest pretensions will still be an ornament in its way and an honor and advantage also to Judaism in this region. Of course, we do not assume or wish to prescribe to our friends what is expected or what we may hope to receive from them in behalf of this enterprise. The object and the circumstances of our Congregation as above referred to will doubtless commend the scheme to your favorable consideration. At all events we most earnestly and hopefully invoke your sympathy and assistance and shall expect, when occasion offers, to reciprocate in a similar manner to such of our brethren as may be found in like circumstances. Any contribution made to us may be remitted to Mr. M. Freud, 11 Harriett Street, Detroit, Michigan, Chairman of the undersigned committee.

On November 12, 1876, the *Detroit Free Press* carried an announcement on behalf of the congregation that the synagogue building and school would be sold at public auction on Tuesday, November 14. The purchaser was expected to remove the building from the property at Congress and St. Antoine within thirty days. The announcement specified that the sale was ordered by the "New Building Committee of the Congregation Shaarey Zedek."

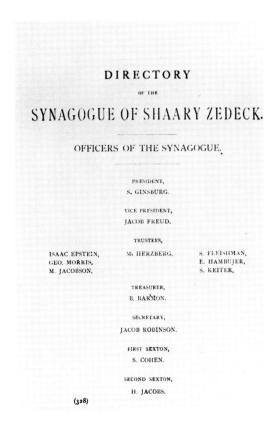

1877 roster of Shaarey Zedek members.

The ceremonies of laying the corner-stone of the new edifice of the Congregation Shaarey Zedeck, of which Rev. Dr. Rosensweig is Rabbi, occurred on Friday morning. The foundation walls were covered with planks, upon which seats were arranged, the speaker's stand being at the northwest corner. The streets were crowded with spectators, while on the platform were between 300 and 400 persons, among them being Mayor Lewis and members of the City Council.

Detroit Free Press, *July 6, 1877*

Synagogue building erected at Congress and St. Antoine site in 1877. The photograph, from Silas Farmer's *History of Detroit and Wayne County and Early Michigan,* published in 1884, probably reproduced the architectural rendering of the building rather than the actual structure; a number of Shaarey Zedek members who attended services there as youths recalled that the building did not have the tall towers shown in Farmer's version.

On Friday, July 4, 1877, the cornerstone of the new building at Congress and St. Antoine was laid. Hundreds of people thronged the streets to watch, and hundreds more stood on the platform, including the mayor and members of the city council. A tin box buried with the cornerstone contained lists of the memberships of Shaarey Zedek and Beth El and their constitutions and by-laws, the Constitution of the State of Michigan, copies of American-Jewish newspapers and Detroit papers of July 3, 1877, a silver Jewish coin and an American coin dated 1877, and the constitution of the Order of B'nai Brith. The mayor himself laid the cornerstone of the first building in Michigan to be erected specifically as a synagogue. All places of Jewish worship before this time had been halls, private homes, or churches remodeled to use as synagogues.

But by the time the synagogue was completed, there was dissension within the congregation. The money to pay for it could not be raised, and Shaarey Zedek was unable to take possession of its new building. The cause of the dissension is unclear. According to some sources, the problem was a financial one, related to the aftermath of the panic of 1873. There was little money in Detroit in the late 1870s, and it was difficult to obtain contributions for the synagogue. Other sources attribute the difficulties to a congregational disagreement over questions of ritual. In any case, the membership splintered into three groups. One met at Kittelberger's Hall on Randolph Street (the Shaarey Zedek group), another at the home of Mr. Kinsell on Gratiot (becoming Congregation Beth Jacob in 1878), and the third met at Funke's Hall on Macomb Street (this group became Congregation B'nai Israel in 1881). Shaarey Zedek was left with only thirty-five members.

Spitzley Brothers, the builders, took a deed for the building, and a mechanic's lien was held by Conrad Clippert, who furnished the brick. The building was unused, and the basement was apparently open to anyone who chose to enter. On Monday night, July 12, 1880, the building was rocked by an explosion. Every pane of stained glass was shattered, the window sashes and casings wrenched away; whole sections of the gallery and main ceiling were blown out. There was a gaping hole in the roof, and the exterior wall was so cracked and forced outward that it was about an inch out of line. The damage was estimated at four thousand dollars. A police investigation discovered an open gas pipe in the basement, pointing to vandalism as the cause of the explosion. On May 12, 1881, the building was sold at auction by Spitzley Brothers and Conrad Clippert. Captain Stephen B. Grummond purchased the building and grounds for $6,775.00 with the intention of tearing it down and replacing it with houses. After a good deal of difficulty, Shaarey Zedek members led by their president, Reuben Mendelsohn, and David W. Simons succeeded in renting the building from Captain Grummond and held services there regularly. By 1884, the membership had doubled and was now able to buy the building for $10,500.00. The building was rededicated on January 17, 1886. In *The Detroit Tribune* of January 18th, the reporter tells us that, following musical renditions, Mr. Ginsburg, one of the trustees, expressed the feeling of the congregation at regaining their synagogue:

> The old saying that there is a silver lining to every cloud we now appreciate and accept. Nine years ago, after a terrific struggle, we succeeded in erecting this structure, and we then felt that we had accomplished an almost impossible task. We took great pride in the fact that we had one of the finest structures for an Orthodox Congregation in the United States. Time rolled on, and about five years after we dedicated it came a vast amount of trouble and anxiety. The sources from which we expected to realize the desired help failed us entirely, and we then found ourselves drifting on the sea of debt. Our rudder was broken, and no sail on the future's horizon cheered our hopes. We felt that all was gone, that all our struggles for years had come to naught. Instead, however, of abandoning hope, we came to the determination to make still another effort. I congratulate you, Mr. President, on the rededication of this, our old "shule," to be held by us forever and forever.

In the 1880s and 1890s, life in Detroit was becoming more modern. Those with telephones would often invite their friends in for a "telephone party"; when the aged mother of a Shaarey Zedek family arrived from Russia, she asked whether one could speak into the new telephone in Yiddish or whether it was intended strictly for American. The early '80s brought electric lighting, although few could afford the cost of some four dollars per month to light a home. Most houses were lit by kerosene or gas. Cordwood was the most common fuel, and a man went from house to house carrying an ax and a saw offering to cut wood into stove lengths for fifty cents a cord. Detroit's wide, beautiful streets, many lined with magnificent mansions, were illuminated in the evening by electric lighting. In an effort to save money, street lighting was generally contracted for on a "moonlight" basis. On nights when the almanac predicted that the moon would shine, the lamps remained unlit no matter how cloudy the night or how dark the streets. The whole town adopted the bicycle. A speed of eleven miles per hour was permitted on Woodward and Jefferson avenues during rush hours, although Detroit's two bicycle-mounted policemen might wink at speeds of up to fifteen miles per hour. There were so many bicycles on the streets of Detroit that it was often difficult for a pedestrian to cross a street when traffic was heavy. Roller skating was in vogue, and the two-day regattas on the river illustrate the popularity of rowing and boating. In its early years, the Detroit Yacht Club had a number of Jewish yachtsmen as members.

Many young men of Shaarey Zedek were interested in debating. Charles Simons, whose talent for oratory was obvious when he was still a Bar Mitzvah boy at Shaarey Zedek at Congress and St. Antoine streets, organized a debating society at Capital High School. As the number of Jewish students in Detroit's high schools

Do you recall Detroit back to 1900?
Back to 1900? I recall back to 1890.

Where did your family live?
Corner of Mullett and Hastings streets.

What was your home like in those days? Did you have electricity?
No. I remember wiping out chimneys with a piece of paper.

Did the family have a telephone?
Only multimillionaires had one. Who could afford two dollars a month? The Wertheimers had one. They were in business, and that is why they had a telephone. We had one thing, though, that we don't have today — the greatest thing of all — peace of mind. The average man made five dollars a week and lived comfortably.

What did a family do for relaxation and recreation?
When we were children we had a family whom we visited every Sunday — a great relaxation was to walk to Belle Isle, eat, and walk back — three or four miles. Who had three cents for carfare?

What did you do after school?
When I was in high school, we went to cheder every day. We studied, and by nine o'clock at night everyone was in bed. There was nothing else to do.

Robert Marwil

When I attended Shaarey Zedek as a boy, I remember Mr. Mendelsohn, who was president, and Mr. Tannenholz.

What kind of place was Tannenholz's saloon?

A high class saloon. Nothing political took place there. He had Jewish trade — a nice clientele.

Robert Marwil

People were coming in from Europe, and they had to be helped. Handkerchief collections were a popular means of fund-raising. People lived close together — and handkerchief collections were done individually; it was not a congregational activity. I remember my mother being very active in this.

William Friedman

increased, it became more and more difficult for them to secure admission to these societies. Despite this, many boys distinguished themselves as debaters — Harry B. Keidan, later to become a prominent jurist, was elected captain of the Eastern High School debating team, although he was the only Jewish member. In September of 1898, a group of Jewish boys, most from Shaarey Zedek, organized the Philomathic Debating Society. Charter members included Louis Wine, Louis Smilansky, Meyer Cohen, Ira Friedenberg, and Morris Smilansky; Hyman Keidan joined the club shortly after it was organized. For years, many of the debates were held at Shaarey Zedek buildings and at the Hannah Schloss Memorial Building.

So content were the citizens of Detroit with their prosperity in the 1880s that they ignored the corruption in city government. Public funds were squandered, and favoritism and nepotism were the order of the day. More political deals were concluded at meetings in the city's saloons than in city offices. The "Liquid Refreshments Dispensing Parlor" at Hastings and Catherine, which belonged to Alexander Tannenholz, president of Congregation Shaarey Zedek in 1889, was said by some to be a popular electioneering spot for politicians of the Second District.

Congregation Shaarey Zedek was in the home it had acquired after years of sacrifice and struggle. During this period of general prosperity, an influx of Russian Jews swelled the Jewish population of Detroit. Unlike their German brethren who had migrated earlier, bringing their possessions, the Russian Jews had fled from pogroms and persecution with very little, and the congregation took the plight of the newly arrived immigrants to its heart. Up to 1885, organized charitable activities in the community were handled primarily through the Beth El Relief Society, with which Shaarey Zedek cooperated closely. But the society and the Shaarey Zedek members disagreed on how to solve the problems posed by the immigrants, forcing Shaarey Zedek members to form the Jewish Relief Society.

In 1883, Louis Bloomgarden, who had previously served the congregation as shochet, was appointed rabbi. Under his guidance the first Sunday School was organized, and the congregation engaged its first cantor. During his stay at Shaarey Zedek, Cantor Wasserczuck changed his name to Winchell; for many years Shaarey Zedek members argued as to whether the nationally known columnist and newscaster Walter Winchell was the grandson of their cantor.

When Aaron M. Ashinsky became the Shaarey Zedek rabbi in 1889, the congregation had grown to over seventy families, yet it was unable to support a rabbi of its own. Rabbi Ashinsky was separately employed by three congregations, Shaarey Zedek, Beth Jacob, and B'nai Israel, leading services alternately in each.

Religious and Hebraic education was the province of private

schools operated by men who were often both inadequately prepared and unsuited to the task. Those cheders of Rabbi Stolarsky and Rabbi Buch were attended by most of Shaarey Zedek's youngsters, who recalled with trepidation the lashings administered by "Red Whiskers" Stolarsky. Recognizing the inadequacy of the cheder system, Rabbi Ashinsky preached the need for a modern educational system, but his efforts to organize a school were unsuccessful.

At this time, Cantor Moses Dlugoff came to Shaarey Zedek. Known as "Babechick," Cantor Dlugoff had sung with a choir at his previous position in Bialystok, and he proceeded to organize a choir for the High Holy Days and special occasions shortly after his arrival. But the congregation could not afford an elaborate choir, and the cantor resigned, returning to Bialystok.

During the 1880s and 1890s several families who were to guide the affairs of the congregation for decades to come assumed active roles in the community. Abe Keidan brought his family to Detroit and opened a clothing store at 600 Gratiot Avenue. Their home above the store was fondly referred to as "Keidan's Depot." The store was closed on the Sabbath. On Saturday evenings, there were often so many shoppers lined up in front waiting for it to open that a policeman was needed to regulate the traffic.

David W. Simons was president of the Hamtramck State Bank, which he had organized. Every Friday, accompanied by one of his sons, Charles or Nathan, he would walk with a yellow bag to the bank to cash the payroll check for the employees of the Griggs Manufacturing Company. When the Public Lighting Commission was organized in 1893, Mr. Simons was appointed a member and later served as its president. Drafted by the Detroit Citizens League to serve on the first nine-man City Council, he served only one term, declining a second because of advancing years and the pressure of business, but the council voted him freedom of the floor for life.

William Saulson had moved to Detroit from St. Ignace, where he had served as mayor, president of the Water Board, and vice-president of the First National Bank of St. Ignace. When he was in St. Ignace, he recognized the need for a bridge to span the straits of Mackinac and attempted to interest his fellow citizens. In Detroit, Mr. Saulson organized the Peerless Manufacturing Company and took an active role in community affairs.

An economic depression engulfed Detroit in 1893, leaving twenty-five thousand workers without jobs. Mayor Hazen Pingree called on owners of vacant property to allow the unemployed to use the land to grow fruits and vegetables. Whole families could be seen planting, hoeing, and weeding. These sites were known as "potato patches," and Mayor Pingree as the "Potato Patch King." The average wage of a laborer in Detroit was $1.62 a day. A loaf of bread was a nickel; a pound of butter was twenty cents. Streetcar

Rabbi Aaron M. Ashinsky, rabbi of Congregation Shaarey Zedek from 1889-1896.

Do you remember Rabbi Stolarsky?
Oh yes, he was the one who used to murder the children. He knew nothing but reading, but we had nobody there but him, and if the children didn't want to read, he would smash them over the head. Some parents gave him a good licking. This is why we built a Talmud Torah, because we didn't want him to bring up our children.

Maurice H. Zackheim

Mr. Keidan had a store on Gratiot between Dequindre and St. Aubin with his son Joe — men's and women's furnishings. On Saturday night people would stand outside and say: "Joe, the stars are out; let's open the store."

Robert Marwil

Members Remember

We lived on the east side. We would go visiting on the west side on Saturday and Sunday, making the same preparations you would if you went on a safari today. We used horsedrawn cars with straw on the floor. The motorman wore a great big bearskin coat, and a ride was five cents. When Mayor Pingree came into office, we had eight tickets for twenty-five cents. For years I never rode on streetcars. Who could afford three cents? In a restaurant a meal consisting of two eggs, two rolls with butter, and two cups of coffee totaled ten cents. We had stoves with base burners — what a job to take out ashes — to clean lights with a piece of newspaper and put oil in them! It didn't seem hard because we didn't know the difference.

Robert Marwil

For a short time there was a cantor by the name of Chaim Wasserczuck. Wasserczuck was a great chazzan, but he had one weakness — he liked winchell, which is cherries soaked in whiskey. Walter Winchell is a grandson of that chazzan. When I met him in Florida, Winchell was sitting with a few reporters and said he was the chazzan's grandson. Wasserczuck (Winchell) was the first cantor — middle of 1880s.

Maurice H. Zackheim

[William] Saulson was a very pious man. He never broke a law affecting either dietetics or the Sabbath, or anything else enjoined upon Jews. At a ceremony of the unveiling of a plaque in his memory, Dr. A. M. Hershman of Congregation Shaarey Zedek, of which Saulson was president 48 years ago, recalled that when this venerable man retired from the mayoralty of St. Ignace, his townsmen came to him and told him that they knew they could not give him a banquet because he disapproved of it. Furthermore, he would have to have special food. Therefore, they proposed that the honor should take this form: Saulson was to name his own successor, and he would be elected unanimously. That actually took place.

Philip Slomovitz in The Jewish News

Meyer Smith, sexton of Congregation Shaarey Zedek, 1890-1915.

1891 invitation to the marriage of Hattie Burnstein to William Lansky; the ceremony was held at Congregation Shaarey Zedek, the reception at Irving Hall on Gratiot Avenue.

Kiddush cup "Presented as a token of esteem by the Members of the Congregation Shaarey Zedeck to the retiring President M. Herzberg."

Congregation Sharey Zedeck.

This Agreement, Made this _____ day of _____ A. D. 189_6

by and between CONGREGATION SHAREY ZEDECK, of _Detroit_ County of _Wayne_

State of Michigan, and _Mr. L. Blumenthal_

of _Detroit_ County of _Wayne_ State of Michigan, witnesseth:

FIRST: That said _Congregation Sharey Zedeck_

sold to _Blumenthal_ the following

described property to wit: _Gents Seat (#34) on Chirty Four Sect. 1_
East Side, Ladies seat (#5) No five, Sect 1, West Side
situated in Synagogue of Congregation Sharey Zedeck
Corner Antoine & Congress Street, City of Detroit

upon and after full payment therefor by said _L. Blumenthal_

of the sum of _One hundred seventy five_ Dollars, in manner following:

Sixty seven 50/67⁵⁰ dollars upon the execution and delivery of this Agreement, _paid to date_

Twelve °° _12_ °° dollars on or before the _First_ day of _Septbr_ A. D. 1890

Twelve °° _12_ °° dollars on or before the _First_ day of _Septbr_ A. D. 1891

Twelve °° _12_ °° dollars on or before the _First_ day of _Septbr_ A. D. 1892

Twelve °° _12_ °° dollars on or before the _First_ day of _Septbr_ A. D. 1893

Twelve °° _12_ °° dollars on or before the _First_ day of _Septbr_ A. D. 1894

Seven °° _7⁵⁰_ dollars on or before the _First_ day of _Septbr_ A. D. 1895

_____ dollars on or before the _____ day of _____ A. D. 1896.

_____ dollars on or before the _____ day of _____ A. D. 1897.

_____ dollars on or before the _____ day of _____ A. D. 1898.

_____ dollars on or before the _____ day of _____ A. D. 1899.

_____ dollars on or before the _____ day of _____ A. D. 1900.

SECOND: That said _L. Blumenthal_ shall and
will pay for said property, said sum of _One hundred twenty five_ °° dollars
at the time and in the manner above mentioned, at the _Office of_
the Congregation in the said _City_ of _Detroit_

THIRD: That the title to said property and the right of possession thereto, shall be and remain in said CONGRE-
GATION SHAREY ZEDECK, until said sum of _One hundred twenty five_ °°
dollars shall be fully paid.

FOURTH: That in case of default in any of the payments of principal, when due as above specified _the_
Congregation shall thereupon forthwith have the right to declare this Contract at an
end, and to take immediate possession of said above described property, and, in such case, the said property, as well as
payments of principal which shall have been made hereon, shall belong to and be retained by said CONGREGATION
SHAREY ZEDECK, as stipulated damages for non-performance of this Contract on the part of said _Blumenthal_

In witness whereof, The parties hereto have hereunto set their hands and seals this _____
_____ day of _October_ A. D. 189_6

_____ PRESIDENT.

H. M. Cohen SECRETARY.

Agreement between Congregation Shaarey
Zedek and Mr. L. Blumenthal regarding the
purchase of two seats in the synagogue at Congress and St. Antoine streets, "Gent's seat"
number thirty-four and "Ladies seat" number
five; the price was $125.00.

fare was three cents, and not everyone could afford to ride. The young people of Shaarey Zedek would hike three or four miles to picnic on Belle Isle to save that three-cent fare.

Rabbi Judah L. Levin, one of the most distinguished spiritual leaders to serve the Jewish community of Detroit, came to the city in 1897 and officiated alternately at Beth Jacob, B'nai Israel, and Shaarey Zedek. His scholarship, character, and dignified bearing endeared him to the congregation and earned their deepest respect; Yeshivah Beth Yehuda is named in his memory. He was a brilliant mathematician as well and invented an early adding machine which was displayed by the Smithsonian Institution and remains in their collection.

Rabbi Ashinsky's dream of a modern religious school was realized in 1898, when Shaarey Zedek and other members of the Jewish community established a Talmud Torah, whose purpose was "to establish, maintain, and control an institution or institutions for the disseminating of religious knowledge, and especially for the purpose of instructing children of the Jewish faith in the history of that religion and its doctrines . . . ." The original Shaarey Zedek supporters included Hyman Buchalter, Samuel and Nathan Ginsburg, David W. Simons, Abraham Jacobs, William Saulson, Samuel Goldstein, and Abe Keidan.

For more than forty years, Isaac Weinstein was the revered baal koreh of the congregation. He was also a mohel. Many a Detroit Jew consulted Mr. Weinstein's painstaking records to determine his exact date of birth.

The influx of Jewish refugees continued. A Jewish community of some 665 individuals in a city of 116,000 in 1880 had grown to over 5,000 Jews in a city of 300,000 in 1900. It was time that the mutual benefit organizations be supplanted by organized philanthropy to look after the needs of the poor, the orphaned, the widowed, and the sick. In 1895, Ben Ginsburg, a Shaarey Zedek trustee, donated a house on Division Street to use as a House of Shelter to care for the poor and sick. During the same year, Joseph Beisman of Shaarey Zedek joined other community leaders in organizing the Hebrew Free Loan Association to give financial assistance to those in need. Membership in the association was solicited among the entire Jewish community, with dues fixed at five cents per week. Initially, only short term loans were extended in amounts not exceeding twenty-five dollars, secured by either collateral or notes bearing two reputable endorsements. No interest or other charges were made.

No Jew ever went hungry or had to brave the rigors of winter without adequate shelter or clothing. No Jew was unattended in illness or alone in sorrow. These needs had been met by a number of individual fraternal and synagogue-sponsored aid societies, each working alone, and the competition for funds and the duplication of effort now appeared unwise. On November 21, 1899, representa-

Rabbi Judah L. Levin, rabbi of Congregation Shaarey Zedek from 1897-1904 and chief rabbi of the United Hebrew Congregations of Detroit, which included Shaarey Zedek, until his death in 1926.

Detroit Hebrew Orphan's Home.

This Indenture,

Made this _Twenty Seventh_ day of _November_ in the year of our Lord one thousand eight hundred and ninety _six_ BETWEEN _Charles Blauck and Christina Blauck his wife of Detroit, County of Wayne State of Michigan_ parties of the first part, and _The Congregation Shaary Zedek a corporation organized under the laws of the State of Michigan_ parties of the second part,

Witnesseth, That the said part _ies_ of the first part, for and in consideration of the sum of _One Thousand_ ——————————— Dollars, to _them_ in hand paid by the said part _ies_ of the second part, the receipt whereof is hereby confessed and acknowledged, do __ by these presents grant, bargain, sell, remise, release, alien and confirm unto the said part _ies_ of the second part, and _their_ heirs and assigns, FOREVER, all _those_ certain piece _ or parcel _ of land situate and being in the _Town_ of _Hamtramack_ County of _Wayne_ and State of Michigan, and described as follows, to-wit:

Beginning at the north east corner of the cemetery formerly deeded to the Congregation Shaary Zedek a corporation by said first parties, being fifty four feet in width on its easterly end exclusive of seven feet for alley purpose and being four hundred and thirteen & xx/100 ft long on its northerly line which is parallel with the southerly line of Hasrahs Brandenburgs Subdivision, South 64° 06' West and fifty three xx/100 feet more on its westerly end & having a southerly line parallel with its said northerly line nearly extending four hundred & thirteen feet. Said premises being particularly described as lot (34) of Blauck's and Hartwigs subdivision of part of quarter section (59) of the 10000 Acre tract Hamtramack Wayne Co, Michigan Dated May 27 1891 when said plat they been duly recorded in Registers office Wayne Co Michigan

Together with all and singular the hereditaments and appurtenances thereunto belonging or in anywise appertaining: **To Have and to Hold** the said premises, as _above_ described, with the appurtenances, unto the said part _ies_ of the second part, and to _their_ heirs and assigns, **Forever.** And the said _Charles Blauck and Christina Blauck his wife_ part _ies_ of the first part, _for their_ heirs, executors and _____ administrators, do covenant, grant, bargain and agree to and with the said part _ies_ of the second part _their_ heirs and assigns, that at the time of the ensealing and delivery of these presents _they are_ well seized of the above granted premises in Fee Simple ; that they are free from all incumbrances whatever

Deed for cemetery property in Hamtramck dated November 27, 1896; conveyance of land adjacent to the Smith Street Cemetery from Charles and Emma Blauck to Congregation Shaarey Zedek. Purchased for one thousand dollars as additional cemetery area, the land was never used by the congregation as Hamtramck was soon incorporated as a city and zoning regulations prohibited this use.

Division Street Talmud Torah.

tives of Shaarey Zedek's Jewish Relief Society met with representatives of the Beth El Hebrew Relief Society, the Hebrew Ladies
Sewing Society, and the Self-Help Circle and founded the United
Jewish Charities, Detroit Jewry's first centralized charitable organization, out of which developed the Jewish Welfare Federation in
1926. David W. Simons was elected president; he was succeeded by
Bernard Ginsburg.

The first classes sponsored by the Talmud Torah Association
had been held in a modest cottage on Division Street. A lot was
purchased at the corner of Division and Beaubien and a handsome
building erected, the first built by Detroit Jews specifically to
house an institution of Jewish learning. Generously endowed by
Bernard Ginsburg, David W. Simons, and Abraham Jacobs, it was
soon to be used by Congregation Shaarey Zedek.

Because the Jewish population was moving northward, it
became necessary to find a new synagogue site. Samuel N. Ginsburg donated a parcel of land on Winder Street between Beaubien
and St. Antoine and plans were being drawn up for a new building
when the opportunity arose to sell the structure at Congress and
St. Antoine. In October of 1901 it was purchased by Homer Warren
for seven thousand dollars. Mr. Warren converted it to a laundry,
prompting a reporter from the *Detroit News-Tribune* to assure his
readers that: "Cleanliness being next to Godliness, the sale of the
old Shaarey Zedek Synagogue that it may be used as a laundry is
not so startling as it may seem at first flash."

For the second time in its history, Shaarey Zedek was without a
home, and arrangements were made for religious services to be
held at the Talmud Torah building.

Hyman Buchalter, principal of the Division
Street Talmud Torah.

35

I remember the Winder Street building had a balcony on the west side, where the women sat. In those days the president and the vice-president always wore silk hats, and ex-presidents as well. D. W. Simons and William Saulson didn't like to wear the silk hats on the street because they felt that they weren't advertising anything. They would leave their silk hats in the basement of the schule. On a couple of occasions the hats just disappeared, either as a prank or stolen, so they decided to take the hats home. Seymour and I used to go ahead with the silk hats, and on the street just before they went into the schule, they would change hats. In those days, it was very formal in the synagogue. On the High Holy Days, they wore cut-away coats, frock coats, and striped trousers. It all lent a great deal of dignity to the congregation and the service.

Sidney R. Jacobs

Do you recall the appearance of the automobile in Detroit around 1905 or 1906?

When I was probably eight years old, which would be 1898, I remember that I skipped school to go to Grosse Pointe, where they had automobile races. There was a Ford car and a Brush car. I know it took me all day to get out there, and I hitched a ride back by horse and buggy.

Abraham Srere

The cornerstone for the new sanctuary on Winder Street was laid on Sunday, June 15, 1902. From the *Detroit Free Press* of the following day, we learn that the hundreds of members who were there were undeterred by the discomfort of "a hot sun that shot its rays downward mercilessly alike upon the just and unjust . . . a score or more of American flags flapped ambitiously in a breeze that did nothing whatever toward the coooling of the atmosphere." A canopy covered the end of the platform farthest from Winder Street, and under this the speakers and a few older members took refuge. Mr. and Mrs. Ginsburg, who had donated the site, were given the honor of laying the cornerstone, accompanied by Abraham Jacobs, the chairman of the building committee. After Rabbi Levin's address, Rabbi Leo M. Franklin delivered a message from Temple Beth El:

> There is no forward movement of the Orthodox congregations in Detroit which Temple Beth El does not regard with pleasure. I am glad to congratulate you because your interests are our interests. The terms "Orthodox" and "Reform" are today vague, and why should we use them when the first congregation regarded as Reform in this city would in some places be considered very Conservative?

That the Winder Street building was soon to be too small for the growing congregation can be understood in the context of the growth of Detroit itself and of the automobile industry. Several Shaarey Zedek members recalled their childhood days when they skipped school to attend automobile races in Grosse Pointe, watching Barney Oldfield drive his "999" to a spectacular triumph. From a small, friendly city, Detroit was in the process of becoming a dynamic metropolis, a world center of big business bustling with activity and employing armies of workers.

The Jewish community had almost no part in the development of the automobile, yet the few instances in which Jews took a leading role in the new industry involved Shaarey Zedek families. The Grabowsky brothers, whose parents' names appear in the congregational roster of 1877, established the Grabowsky Power Wagon Company in Pontiac to manufacture self-propelled wagons. They sold their small factory to Will Durant, who added it to the rapidly growing chain which was to become General Motors; Joshua Grabowsky joined General Motors. The Mendelsohn brothers were active in a company which manufactured automobile bodies, later known as the Fisher Body Company. Louis Mendelsohn served as treasurer and chairman of the Board of Directors, while Aaron was secretary.

A decade later, another Shaarey Zedek member played an important role in the automotive industry: Meyer L. Prentis. Prentis, who was involved in congregational affairs from the time he came into the community in 1911 through the early 1920s, was the auditor for the Laclede Gas Light Company of St. Louis, where he was known as a man of limitless energy and great ability. He was

Program of the dedication of the Winder Street synagogue, March 1, 1903. After Samuel N. Ginsburg lit the perpetual light and the key was presented to President Alexander Tannenholz, an address was delivered by Rabbi Judah L. Levin.

invited by General Motors to come to Detroit; in 1911 he was appointed chief accountant and in 1919 became the treasurer.

The new synagogue on Winder Street was dedicated on Sunday afternoon, March 1, 1903. Twelve of the oldest members of the congregation marched around the synagogue bearing the sacred scrolls of the Torah before they were deposited in the ark. Cantor Moses Rogoff chanted the twenty-first psalm, followed by "Open the Gates of Righteousness," from which the congregation had originally selected its name of Shaarey Zedek, or "Gates of Righteousness."

The Renaissance interior of the synagogue featured a main auditorium fifty-seven feet square finished in oak and plaster work. The galleries and semi-circular pews seated seven hundred and fifty, farsighted planning for a congregation of forty-five families.

There are in Detroit hundreds of Jews that were born in Russia and have been subjected to persecutions similar to those suffered by the Jews there today. Some of them came from the districts where the terrible massacres recently occurred.

The bloodshed in Russia has aroused sympathy all over the world for the victims and emigration from Russia is expected to be heavier than usual this year. Many of these people who leave their native land to find peace, liberty and happiness come to the United States, and they are to be found in nearly all the large cities.

In New York city there is a large colony of them that includes men who are prominent in law, medicine, business and music. There is also the Ghetto, where the poorest and most ignorant have settled.

The condition of the Jews in the Ghetto has caused some people to say that they are not desirable immigrants, the allegation being made that most of them come here almost paupers.

These Have Prospered

It is interesting in this connection to learn about those Russian Jews in Detroit who come here without money and now hold positions of prominence throughout the city. Some of them have been here only eight or ten years; others have been here thirty years or more. Among them we find several who are known to be worth several hundred thousand dollars, and at least one who is worth in the neighborhood of a million.

Not only have they been successful in acquiring wealth by legitimate business methods, but others have attained prominence in law, medicine and music. They came here without money, without education and without influential friends. What they have they earned by their energy, their perseverance and their native ability. They occupy fine, large, well-furnished houses in the fashionable streets and avenues, and some of these Jews have been honored with political positions by their fellow-men.

These men are well-known by their fellow-citizens. They are interested in many business enterprises with men who were born in Detroit and their co-operation is invited when new enterprises are proposed. They have done much in educational and charitable affairs, and they are good citizens.

All Good Citizens

There are a large number of Russian Jews in Detroit who have not prospered so well in business, but they are making their way upward. There are others who are not so well educated and who have to work hard for a living, like some of their fellowmen of other races, but they are peaceful, law-abiding citizens. Look through the reports of prisons and similar institutions and you will find few Jews and very few Russian Jews, in proportion to men and women of other religions. They do not get drunk and disturb the peace on the streets. There are few criminals of any kind among them. They make good citizens, men who believe in having homes of their own, and men who think much of the home life.

The Russian Jews must not be looked down upon because they came from another country, for all of us or our ancestors have been in the position of immigrants some time since 1492. The names of some of the Jews who were born in Russia and have attained prominence in this city and state are a sufficient argument that Russian Jews are a desirable class of immigrants.

William Saulson, secretary and treasurer of the Peerless Manufacturing Co. on East Larned street, between Bates and Randolph streets, formerly lived at St. Ignace, where he was mayor, vice-president of the First National bank, and president of the water board. He lives at 111 Edmund Place.

D. W. Simons, formerly a member of the public lighting commission, is a well-known real estate dealer at 604 Wayne County bank building.

Louis J. Rosenberg, of Gates & Rosenberg, attorneys, Home bank building, is also an author. He lives at 311 Brush street.

S. Ginsburg, of Ginsburg & Son, is the head of a large iron business having contracts with the New York Central and other large railroad companies. He was poor like the rest when he came here, but today he is reported to be worth close to a million. He lives at 80 Adelaide street.

Abraham Jacobs is the founder of the East Side Electric Co., and is interested in many other business enterprises. His home is at 52 Alfred street.

A. Simon, of 33 Alfred street, is the head of the firm of A. Simon & Co., dealers in paper mill supplies, located at 203-213 Beaubien street. He is understood to be wealthy, and has a very artistically and richly furnished home.

Dr. N. E. Aronstam is a professor of the Michigan College of Medicine, and was Michigan delegate to the British congress on tuberculosis in 1901. He is an author, and with Louis J. Rosenberg has published a book entitled "Sociologic Studies." He lives at 164 East High street.

Dr. Joseph Beisman, whose office is in the Arcade, is another of the successful Jews that were born in the czar's domains.

A. Marymont, wholesale liquor dealer.

Dr. I. L. Polozker, county physician; his office is in the Homer Warren building.

Max J. Rosenberg, of 42 West Larned street, book binder.

Joseph Rosenzweig is in the iron business.

M. Mitshkun is in the railway equipment business, in the Chamber of Commerce building.

Boris L. Ganapol, the well-known singer and teacher, whose studio is in the Valpey building, lives at 39 East Canfield avenue.

This list might be considerably lengthened, as there are a number of other Russian Jews in Detroit who are well-known, and who are prominent in business and the professions. It is said that of the 5,000 Jewish families in Detroit, two-thirds are Russian or Roumanian.

Why They Stay in the Cities

One of the great objections that has been raised by some against the Jews from Russia is that they do not at once go out into the country and become farmers, or go to work in factories. The Russian Jews who live in Detroit say that it is hardly to be expected that the first generation will do this, for the reason that they have been kept from such work all their lives by the Russian government. In fact, the whole story of the mean laws and regulations put in force in Russia to keep the Jews down would hardly be believed in this free country.

The Jews in Russia cannot live in villages or cities, unless they were born there. They cannot own real

THE DETROIT FREE PRESS, May 31, 1903

estate of any kind. They cannot work on a farm of a Greek churchman unless there is no Christian labor to be obtained. The right to get an education has been so hedged as to be prohibitive. The only occupations that the Jews are permitted to engage in are petty and allow them to make only enough for a mere existence, in most cases.

Helping Their Fellow Countrymen

The Russian Jews in America are doing much to relieve the condition of the Jews in New York city. Millions have been spent to educate and aid these people in the last few years. Mr. Rosenberg is now the Michigan superintendent for the Industrial removal office, of New York. This is a national organization, which takes Jews from the Ghetto and brings them west to work on farms or in cities, and positions are provided for them when they arrive. He was also superintendent of the United Jewish charities of Detroit and is a director and member of the Society for the Prevention of Cruelty to Children.

After the Russian Jews have learned the English language and realize that they are free to enter any occupation they choose, they advance quickly. They have been accustomed for generations in Russia to be hemmed in and persecuted, and it is difficult for them to comprehend the great liberties they have in this country. But one of the best signs is that they do not take advantage of these liberties.

Fine Achievements

In Detroit the Russian Jews have accomplished much. They have built four synagogues, the Sha'are Zedek, Beth Israel, Beth Ja'acob and Beth David. They have built the Talmud Torah institute on Division street, where Jews learn the English language and learn to read in Hebrew the rich literature of their race. A House of Shelter has been established on Division street by Russian Jews where the very poor can get meals and lodgings free.

There is a loan office, where Russian Jews can obtain small loans without interest. Michael Davis, born in Russia, is the president of this organization.

It is very apparent that the Russian Jews are able to take care of themselves and of one another, if they are given the opportunity. They are intelligent, sensible, hard-working people, sober and religious, of good moral character and determined to get ahead in the world. They are men with characteristics that make any nation strong.

Rabbi Rudolph Farber, rabbi of Congregation Shaarey Zedek from 1904-1907; born in Austria, Rabbi Farber was trained in rabbinical schools in Bohemia.

When Mr. Saulson was president, he wanted an English-speaking rabbi. Rabbi Farber was a Hungarian and a shochet, too. Cantor Rogoff was a scholar, a talmudist, and a competent musician. He received eight hundred dollars a year, and he knew that if he asked for another hundred dollars, he would have been fired. There was a choir only for the High Holy Days.

Maurice H. Zackheim

When William Saulson became president of the congregation in 1903, his immediate concern was the growing apathy of the younger generation, who felt little kinship with the German-language sermons or with religious patterns geared to the needs of older, European-bred members. Mr. Saulson set out to win them to the synagogue and advised hiring an English-speaking rabbi who would be able "to appeal to the young in their own tongue." On January 22, 1904, Rabbi Rudolph Farber delivered his first sermon, in which he recognized the needs of the younger members, adding that they could be met within the framework of traditional Judaism. Rabbi Farber reorganized the Sunday School and inaugurated Friday evening lectures which were very popular. Shortly after his arrival, a boys' choir under the guidance of Cantor Rogoff was formed, and congregational singing was introduced into the services. Classes in Talmud met daily and on Saturdays between the afternoon Mincha and the evening Maariv services. As new vigor was infused into congregation life, attendance increased among old and young alike.

The congregation began to assume an active role in community charitable work. On October 1, 1906, it voted an appropriation of $586.00 to support the Talmud Torah, the United Jewish Charities, and other educational and charitable institutions. In the same year, the women of Shaarey Zedek formed the Ladies' Auxiliary, later known as the Sisterhood, dedicating their efforts to preserving the traditions of Judaism and to the moral and spiritual development of Shaarey Zedek members. The initial impetus for this organization was the need for new curtains for the ark; throughout the years it has raised funds for equipment and for the beautification of the synagogue.

Within a few years, the new spirit of 1904 had disappeared. The younger members seemed indifferent, and there was a general feeling of dissatisfaction. In April of 1907, Rabbi Farber resigned, and the congregation decided to hire a rabbi who was a graduate of The Jewish Theological Seminary of America, Rabbi Abraham M. Hershman. It was not long before the congregation felt the impact of Rabbi Hershman's forceful personality. The new rabbi established a congregational school, reorganized the Sunday School, and organized a Young People's Society and the Kadimah Society for the study of Jewish history.

An ardent Zionist, Rabbi Hershman not only founded the Detroit branch of the Zionist Federation of America but wrote pamphlets explaining the Zionist movement and collected funds as well.

In the years between 1900 and 1910, almost one million Jewish immigrants came to the United States, many to Detroit. Thus, the Shaarey Zedek building which in 1903 far exceeded the congregation's needs was too small just five years later.

Presidents of the Ladies' Auxiliary/Sisterhood
of Congregation Shaarey Zedek, 1906-1934;
Mrs. David W. Simons (insert), Mrs. Max
Wolstein, Mrs. David Zemon, Mrs. Sol
Kaufman, Mrs. Herbert H. Warner, Mrs.
Maurice H. Zackheim, Mrs. Charles A. Smith,
Mrs. Joseph Zechman.

Sunday School class, 1912; the teacher was
Theresa Meister. Some of those who have been
identified are Sara Caplan, Esther Goldstein,
Rosa Morris, Mr. Horwitz, Miss Jacobson,
Helen Esser, Esther Berman, and
Lillian Solomon.

41

Congregation Shaarey Zedek

WINDER STREET
BETWEEN ANTOINE AND BEAUBIEN STREETS

A. Benjamin, Secretary
566 BRUSH STREET

Detroit, July 5 — 1911

Mr Chas Smith,
221 E. High St.
City,

Dear Sir:—

I beg to inform you that at a meeting held by Congregation Shaarey Zedek July 2nd 1911, your application for membership was Submitted, the same was received, and you was duly elected as a member of the above said Congregation,

Your dues was fixed, until further notice at $15.00 per annum, which is payable quarterly in advance, commencing from July 1st 1911.

Trusting that your affilliation with the Cong, will add another earnst Co-worker for the cause of true Judaism. I beg to remain

Yours Very truly,
A Benjamin
Secretary.

Letter dated July 5, 1911, from A. Benjamin, secretary of Congregation Shaarey Zedek, to Charles Smith, informing Mr. Smith that his application for membership in the synagogue located on Winder Street had been accepted and that his dues would be fifteen dollars per year, payable quarterly in advance.

The Winder Street synagogue.

"I think that the synagogue became more of a center of Jewish activities in Detroit when the Willis Street synagogue was complete because it had facilities for Bar Mitzvah, weddings, and celebrations of a like nature."

Sidney R. Jacobs

Any person of the Jewish faith and of good moral character, of the age of eighteen years or over, who wishes to become a member of the congregation, must apply in writing therefore to the Executive Board, and pay an entrance fee of ten dollars from the age of 18 to 50 years, and of twenty-five dollars from the age of 50 years and upwards. Such application shall lie over one month before being balloted upon. It shall require a majority vote to elect.

1904 By-Laws, Article XIII, Section 1

Mr. William Saulson said in his farewell address of 1908:

Never before did we witness such large assemblies at all the Services. Never before were we obliged to close our doors to those who desired to attend Services. Much to our regret, we were compelled to do so on account of the lack of accommodations, and the membership roster continues to grow. Congregation Shaarey Zedek has outgrown its place of worship and its school. We can no longer say to those who exclaim "Open the gates of righteousness" that the gates are open to all who seek communion with God. There is one great pressing need which must be recognized by all and that is more commodious quarters in which to worship and to teach our children. I therefore would recommend that you authorize the Board of Trustees to act with full power to bring about the great necessity of a commodious school and a larger seating capacity in our place of worship to enable us to go on with our ideal work for faith, knowledge, and truth.

The congregation had grown from forty-five families to almost two hundred, quadrupling its membership in five years.

In 1908, David W. Simons was elected president of the congregation. When he retired in 1920, Shaarey Zedek members made him their first honorary president in recognition of the leadership and devotion to Judaism which gave the synagogue new status in the Detroit community.

The congregation now looked for a location which would serve its needs "for generations to come." In 1910 a site was purchased at the corner of Willis and Brush, and the congregation was again involved in raising funds and planning a new structure. Some members doubted that the congregation could successfully undertake a major financial commitment so soon after paying for the existing synagogue. When approached for contributions, many sought assurance that their pledges would really make the erection of a new synagogue possible and not be used for other purposes.

Ceremony at Willis and Brush. Among those on the platform were Rabbi Abraham M. Hershman, Rabbi Judah L. Levin, David W. Simons, Harry B. Keidan, Louis Granet, Isaac Shetzer, Isaac Saulson, Louis Smith, and Jacob Friedberg.

Program of the cornerstone laying ceremony at Willis and Brush, November 16, 1913.

You are cordially invited
to attend the

Cornerstone Laying Ceremonies

of the new

Shaarey Zedek Synagogue

Sunday afternoon at 2 o'clock

Nov. 16, 1913   Heshvan 16, 5674

at the northwest corner of

Willis Avenue and Brush Street

The preamble to the legal document which listed pledges carefully stated: "We the undersigned hereby pledge ourselves to pay the sum or sums of money set forth opposite our name for the purpose of building larger quarters for the Congregation Shaarey Zedek; said sum or sums of money will become payable on demand in three installments as soon as twenty thousand dollars is subscribed or pledged." The contributions listed ranged from five to twenty-five hundred dollars.

The cornerstone of the new synagogue was laid on Sunday afternoon, November 16, 1913. After an invocation delivered by Rabbi Judah L. Levin, the children of the Shaarey Zedek Sunday School sang a hymn, and addresses were delivered by David W. Simons, Rabbi Leo M. Franklin of Temple Beth El, Jacob Nathan, president of the Young People's Society, and Rabbi Abraham M. Hershman. The honor of laying the cornerstone was given to David W. Simons, Abraham Jacobs, A. Benjamin, and Louis Smith.

When the cornerstone was laid, Shaarey Zedek had reached another milestone in its history as well: it became one of the founding members of the United Synagogue of America, organized under the aegis of Prof. Solomon Schecter to advance the cause of Judaism in America and to maintain Jewish tradition while, at the same time, initiating changes compatible with the times.

The new, Italian Renaissance-style synagogue was dedicated on Sunday, December 5, 1915. Planned to seat 1,432 members in the main sanctuary, it included a large school auditorium, numerous classrooms, a social hall, and a gymnasium.

The old Smith Street Cemetery had long been inadequate. In the 1890s, the congregation had purchased an adjoining parcel of land, but soon after the purchase, the area was incorporated as the city of Hamtramck, and zoning regulations of the new city prohibited the use of the additional land. Shaarey Zedek and a number of other congregations shared the Machpelah Cemetery, but there were disagreements on matters of policy. In 1917, Shaarey Zedek purchased fifty acres of land on Fourteen Mile Road east of Woodward, which is now the Clover Hill Park Cemetery, its rolling terrain punctuated with gardens, trees, an artificial lake, and a chapel.

The United States was in the midst of a world war. Some two thousand Michigan Jews, among them many of Shaarey Zedek's youth, fought on every front. Detroit Jews pledged to contribute thirty-five hundred dollars to the Detroit Patriotic Fund for war relief work. "We must do even more," wrote Rabbi Hershman in a message to the congregation. "We must give not only as Jews but also as men and as Americans."

Under the presidency of Mrs. Wolf Kaplan, the Shaarey Zedek Sisterhood converted the basement rooms of the synagogue into hospital sewing rooms in which almost every member worked to prepare bandages and similar items for the Red Cross. In 1920, the Chevra Kadisha was organized by Isaac Shetzer, Samuel Friedman,

CORNER STONE OF BEAUTIFUL JEWISH TEMPLE LAID TOMORROW

The Detroit News, November 15, 1913.

My father thought that the congregation should have larger quarters and go out farther from Winder Street. A great many people felt that the Winder Street building was the last word. There was an opportunity to buy a piece of land on Willis and Brush, which then was considered quite far out. There was a lot of opposition. People said that my father would never raise the money. He said to a few, "If you can raise twenty thousand dollars, I will be able to raise the rest." So an agreement was drawn on the back of a piece of Charles Simon's stationery.

Sidney R. Jacobs

Dedication ceremony program, Willis and Brush synagogue, December 4-7, 1915.

The synagogue at Willis and Brush; built in the style of the Italian Renaissance with an octagonal dome over the main auditorium at the east end of the building, the synagogue was simple, yet elegant. The carefully crafted details included olive green wainscoting, tile floors, and a ceiling of carved plaster in the lobby; Vermont marble used for the bima reading desk, the pulpit, and colonnades flanking the ark; pews, furniture, and polished oak floors finished in a warm Austrian gray.

Dedication Exercises

Sunday, Kislev 28, at 2:30 p. m.

"PISCHOO LI SHAAREY ZEDEK"

פתחי לי שערי צדק

Open Ye Unto Me the Gates of Richteousness

Procession of the Scrolls

"Mah Tovoo" מה טבו אהליך—How goodly are thy tents, O Jacob! thy Tabernacles, O Israel! And in the greatness of thy benevolence, will I enter thy house..Cantor and Choir

Receiving the Scrolls

Opening the Ark.............................Mr. A. Jacobs
Vice-President of the Congregation

Placing the Scrolls

"Uvnoocha Yomar" ובנחה יאמר—And when the Ark rested, he said, Restore tranquility to the many thousands of Israel...............................Cantor and Choir

Closing the Ark..........................Mr. J. Friedberg
Treasurer of the Congregation

Invocation.................................Rabbi J. L. Levin

Presentation of the Key.........................Mr. A. Klein
Chairman Ways and Means Committee

Acceptance of the Key....................Mr. D. W. Simons
President of the Congregation

Psalm 43—3rd and 4th Verses—Oh send out thy light and thy truth; let them lead me; let them bring me unto thy holy hill, and to thy Tabernacles.
Then will I go unto the altar of God, unto God my exceeding joy; yea upon the harp will I praise thee, O God, my God...............................Cantor and Choir

Lighting the Perpetual Light...........Rabbi A. M. Hershman
Of Congregation Shaarey Zedek

Address.........................Rabbi Leo M. Franklin
Of Congregation Beth El

Presentation of the Golden Book................Jacob Nathan
On behalf of Young People's Auxiliary

Dedication Sermon...................Rabbi A. M. Hershman

Psalm 122—I was glad when they said unto me, Let us go into the house of the Lord..............Cantor and Choir

Lighting the Chanukah Candles..........................

"Mo'oz Tsur Yeshuothi" מעוז צור ישתועי—The strength of the rock of my salvation.................Cantor and Choir

Benediction.........................Rabbi Ezekiel Aushiskin

Reception by officers of the congregation in the school room

Cantor, Bernhard Wladowsky, and Choir, of Toronto

Chapel at Clover Hill Park Cemetery.

and others. The Chevra Kadisha aided bereaved families, comforting them and taking care of necessary business details, giving financial as well as spiritual aid if it was needed.

A Hebrew school had been operated by the congregation; all Jewish children were admitted without charge, but the cost had become a serious drain on congregational resources, and this, coupled with the modifications which would have to be made in the building to meet health and safety requirements, forced the Education Committee to recommend in 1921 "the discontinuance of our daily Hebrew school until such time as Congregation Shaarey Zedek is able to provide the proper and adequate facilities necessary to take care of the needs of the children of our entire membership body." Rabbi Hershman cautioned that a synagogue without a daily school "is a most tragic thing," but the congregation saw that another move was imminent, and major expenditures in its present building appeared to be unwarranted.

By 1917, the membership of Shaarey Zedek had grown to four hundred families, but most of them now lived in the Twelfth Street area. The youth was drifting away again, neither attending services nor taking part in congregation-sponsored activities, and the synagogue at Willis and Brush had become a center for recreational and cultural activities for the neighborhood rather than a center for Shaarey Zedek members. In the early 1920's, within six years of the dedication of the sanctuary at Willis and Brush which was erected "to serve the congregation for generations to come," changing residential areas forced the congregation to consider yet again a new location for the synagogue.

47

Photograph taken on the steps of the synagogue at Willis and Brush.

II. Chicago Boulevard
1922-1960

The war had ended, and Detroit industry had adjusted to a peace-time economy. There was ever-increasing optimism, reflected in new styles of social conduct and dress. Women wore straight, boyish silhouettes with waistlines at the hip and hemlines near the knee and bobbed their hair. In the 1920s, Detroit gained half a million residents and became the fourth largest city in America. Feverish construction of large, impressive buildings inflated values to the point where they lost all touch with reality. During this period, the forty-seven-story Penobscot Building and the Fisher Building were erected; the Detroit-Windsor tunnel and the Ambassador Bridge connected Detroit with its Canadian neighbor across the river. Automobile production exceeded four million units a year.

In 1922, when supplementary services on the High Holy Days were held in the Westminster Community Building in the new Jewish neighborhood, Shaarey Zedek had every reason to share in the general enthusiasm; money was plentiful, and there was reason to expect that it would become even more plentiful. At an informal meeting on March 27, 1922, Samuel Rabinowitz initiated plans for a new synagogue building by pledging two thousand dollars toward the purchase of a lot. The discussions of both the Board of Trustees and the members at large reflected the general optimism.

There was a consensus that the new main sanctuary should seat twenty-five hundred to three thousand, and that the synagogue should include a smaller sanctuary seating five hundred, a chapel for daily services seating one hundred, a hall for meetings and entertainment with a capacity of one thousand, a dining room for twelve hundred, a gymnasium, sixteen classrooms, a library, offices, and facilities for the Men's Club and the Sisterhood.

The well-known architectural firm of Albert Kahn was engaged to draw preliminary sketches and to estimate the cost of such a structure. Mr. Kahn indicated that the cost would be some seven hundred fifty thousand dollars.

"It is the duty and responsibility of Shaarey Zedek," said Harry B. Keidan when confronted with the estimate, "to have a synagogue and a suitable social and educational center. If what is needed can be gotten for four hundred thousand dollars, well enough; if not, let us spend seven hundred fifty thousand dollars. In this question it is vital that the congregation refrain from taking a narrow-minded stand." "It would be just as easy," said another board member, "to raise seven hundred fifty thousand dollars as three hundred thousand dollars. The new structure should be one which will further the purposes of Conservative Judaism; if properly conducted, every facility which will be included in the new synagogue will pay handsomely in social and spiritual dividends."

In November of 1925, a decision was made to purchase property at Chicago Boulevard and Lawton from the Catholic Diocese of Detroit. As soon as it was known that a synagogue was to be

[On April 10, 1922, as the Board of Trustees was considering reports pertaining to sites for a new building at one of its monthly meetings, a young man, his face half-covered with a handkerchief, burst into the room and ordered the trustees to give him their money and jewelry. Several days later the robber, one Morris Greeson, known as the "Cockney Thug" because he had a British accent, was caught after another robbery and identified by four of the trustees.]

I was one of the people at that Board meeting. I can see where everyone was sitting. I came with Isaac Shetzer in a taxi to the meeting. Mr. Srere was there. We sat down — there was always a boy who brought in ice water. He tapped on the door (it was locked) and this man came in and said: "This is a hold-up. I want you to throw out all your money." He was a young man about twenty-one or twenty-two years old. I had fifty dollars that I had just withdrawn from the bank, and I threw it out. He then asked for our watches. Isaac Shetzer said: "Before I left home, my mother gave this to me, and I prize it above everything." I told the same story, and he let us keep our watches. I was not afraid — the thief was more scared than we were. His gun kept shaking in his hand. Then there was another knock on the door, and it was the boy with the ice water. We told him to put it down. We felt that he was in cahoots with the other fellow. Several of the men, I recall, couldn't sleep all night, but I slept.

Robert Marwil

Of course, there were dissenting voices raised, objections to moving the congregation to Chicago Boulevard. Then one of the very senior members spoke. "I have belonged to many congregations and been active in the day-to-day affairs of my synagogue. But this is the first time that I have been blessed with the opportunity to help in planning a building for my children and for my children's children." From that moment, it became clear that the new building would be a reality.

Laying of the cornerstone for the Chicago Boulevard synagogue on May 26, 1930. *Second from the left:* David W. Simons, president of the congregation, is shown holding a trowel; *second from the right:* Rabbi Abraham M. Hershman.

erected, property owners in the neighborhood filed the first of several lawsuits, each ably defended by William Friedman. The first lawsuit concerned the congregation's petition to reroute the alley which ran from Lawton to Wildemere, which was a necessary adjunct to the plans of the new building. The petition and the ensuing lawsuit ran the gamut of decisions from the Detroit City Council to the United States Supreme Court. In each instance, the right of the congregation to proceed was upheld.

Encouraged by the Supreme Court decision, the Board moved on March 7, 1927, that the Albert Kahn organization be authorized to begin excavation work and proceed with plans for construction of the building. However, Kahn was asked to revise the plans so that the cost would not exceed five hundred thousand dollars. Rabbi Hershman broke ground for the new building on March 23, 1927; following his brief address, he pulled the lever which started the steam shovels working on the excavation.

Two days after the excavations had begun, another lawsuit was initiated which claimed that the erection of a synagogue was a violation of local building restrictions, and again the congregation

Religious School
Congregation Shaarey Zedek

Commencement Exercises

Sunday, June 13, 1926
11 A. M.

Program of Shaarey Zedek religious school commencement exercises, June 13, 1926, which included introductory remarks by A. Louis Gordon, superintendent; musical selections played by Abraham Epstein, Charles Rice, and Emma Lazaroff Shaver; a speech given by Eiga Hershman, president of the class of '26; "From an Alumnus," by Samuel Kellman; and an address delivered by Rabbi Abraham M. Hershman.

CONGREGATION
SHAAREY ZEDEK
❖

Laying of the Cornerstone Ceremony

OF THE NEW
SHAAREY ZEDEK SYNAGOGUE

SUNDAY, MAY 25, 1930
2:30 P. M. SHARP

———

CHICAGO BOULEVARD AND LAWTON AVE.
DETROIT, MICHIGAN

Program of the cornerstone laying ceremony of the Chicago Boulevard synagogue, May 26, 1930. Speakers were Shaarey Zedek president A. Louis Gordon, Rabbi Leo M. Franklin of Temple Beth El, and Rabbi Abraham M. Hershman. Rabbi E. Aishiskin of Congregation Beth David gave the closing prayer.

1929 Sunday School class.

From Willis and Brush the synagogue went to Twelfth Street?

Yes — upstairs. If you stood outside the synagogue and smoked a cigarette on the Sabbath, it was very bad. We were there just temporarily. My father, who did not ride, of course, came down and stayed at my house for Yom Kippur because they were raising money on Kol Nidre night, and my father then talked all during Yom Kippur from the time he ate until he broke his fast. He wanted to find out what happened at the synagogue — whether they raised any money.

Dora Ehrlich

was involved in litigation. But the case was won, and at long last the construction of the synagogue could proceed.

In 1929 the Great Depression struck. In its dark hours the congregation shared the experience of the community, and, as the number of unemployed rose from day to day, plans for the building were revised. Albert Kahn was authorized to seek bids and proceed with the main auditorium and the basement provided that the cost was not more than three hundred thousand dollars.

Some two thousand people gathered in a large tent on Sunday afternoon, May 26, 1930, to join David W. Simons in laying the cornerstone of the new synagogue. Rabbi Hershman delivered the major address, in which he stressed the significance of the synagogue. ''No institution in Israel is fraught with more far-reaching possibilities than the synagogue. It is the cornerstone on which the edifice of the entire Jewish life has rested for some eighteen hundred years. We have no substitute for it. If you tamper with this Jewish cornerstone, the entire structure goes down. Without it Jewish activities may continue for a while carried by their own momentum, but not for long.'' The construction was now under way. The building at Willis and Brush was rented to the Mt. Olive Baptist Church, and the congregation held its services in the building it had leased on Twelfth and Clairmount, with supplementary services on the High Holy Days held in a building at Hamilton and Glynn.

Although the new building occupied a major share of the congregation's attention, its programs and activities continued. The Young People's Society was particularly active, attempting to

54

A Shaarey Zedek religious school class of June, 1930, poses with their teacher, Mr. Rogvoy.

develop programs which would attract interested members who would later assume leadership positions in the congregation. Leonard Sidlow, a future president of Shaarey Zedek, led the society in the early 1930s. The Young People's Society catered to young men and women over twenty-one, but there was also a need for an organization to accommodate college-age members. In 1930, the Junior Young People's Society, open to sons and daughters of members between eighteen and twenty-one, was organized, and a varied program of activities begun.

On September 20, 1930, nostalgia prompted many members of Shaarey Zedek to gather at the southeast corner of St. Antoine and Congress to see their first congregational home reduced to empty window frames, showers of plaster, and the dust of crumbling brick and stone.

Funds were now scarce. The contractors advised the Board that they would have to stop construction unless they received a large payment at once. On July 23, 1930, the congregation approved the placing of a ten-year mortgage of two hundred thousand dollars with interest at six percent per annum on the property at Chicago Boulevard to raise funds for construction. The personal guarantees of almost three hundred thousand dollars signed by Shaarey Zedek members reflected their faith in the future of Shaarey Zedek.

Much could be written describing the problems of the congregation of this period and even more about the loyalty and sacrifice of its members, under the leadership of their courageous and indomitable president, A. Louis Gordon. An appeal by President Gordon to the members illustrates the gravity of the situation:

Mixed seating created quite a fuss. They decided to have so many rows. There were just a few families that objected to mixed seating, so they finally took five or six rows to start with — for a long time there were complaints. We were supposed to be Conservative and what we were was Orthodox. You hear the same complaints today.

Abraham Srere

I have been a member of Shaarey Zedek for twenty-two years and your president for two years. Numerically the synagogue has grown from a membership of 531 to 625. You have made a great demonstration within the past two years of the power that lies in cooperation between Jews. You have become increasingly convinced of two great truths. First, that "no man liveth to himself" and the less he tries to do that, the more truly and fully he lives. Second, that no sacred task can fail; buildings devoted to the service of God will rise despite all obstacles. It is almost literally true that every man who owns property is poorer today than he was a year ago; but to the extent that his possessions are represented by his membership or subscription to Shaarey Zedek he is as rich today as he was a year ago. Your investment in the synagogue cannot shrink, nor can it be lost; it is imperishable and returns spiritual dividends to everyone at all time. In making up our balance sheet, the imponderable assets of increase in Jewishness and Jewish spirit far outweigh other things.

Dedication ceremonies for the new synagogue were held on January 9 and 10, 1932. In the address given by Dr. Louis Finkelstein of The Jewish Theological Seminary of America, he spoke of the struggles of the Jew to overcome opposition: "It was the historic resistance to prejudice and persecution that was the basis for the strength which made occasions such as this dedication possible."

The move to Chicago Boulevard seemed to be a good time to institute some changes in synagogue practices which had been championed by many members for some years, changes which had been taking place in Conservative congregations throughout the country. Many families wanted to sit together during services and objected to the old tradition of separating the sexes. In April of 1931, the by-laws were altered, permitting mixed seating in the sanctuary and also providing for a section which was to be reserved for those who wished to follow the Orthodox tradition. And there was another change. The congregation had always recognized the money a member gave to the synagogue by assigning the most desirable seats to those who gave the largest contributions. There had always been a great deal of status connected with the seats closest to the front. Although this may have prompted a good many sizeable contributions, in the new synagogue the entire sanctuary was given over to open seating.

The move to a new sanctuary, usually an occasion for great joy, came at a particularly difficult time in the lives of both Shaarey Zedek and the community. Fifteen million Americans were unemployed, and hungry Detroiters rioted, demanding work. The optimism of the '20s had become the despair of the '30s.

The impact of the Depression on Shaarey Zedek members can be seen in the many requests for the reduction of dues, the cancellation of past due accounts, and the large number of resignations by those who could not pay even nominal charges and preferred not to ask the Board for special favors. One gets the feeling that almost every member required some financial consideration during this period.

The treasurer's report for the period ending March 31, 1932, stated that the congregation had a balance on hand of $247.26 and approximately $10,000.00 in unpaid bills, which included several months of salary due to the rabbi and the cantor, "which we had no money to pay for." During the previous six months, the Ways and Means Committee had carefully investigated the members' accounts to determine which members could pay dues for the year. They did not charge those whom they felt could not pay. Thus, it was imperative that members who had received bills pay their dues. "Those members who have not paid their dues for the first six months are therefore the direct cause of our being behind in the Rabbi's salary and running expenses of the Congregation."

A pamphlet sent to the members in 1932 emphasized the need for funds.

> The present building was constructed as it now stands because a large majority of the membership wanted it so. As many of the facilities as are present are there because the congregation wanted them. YOUR officers provided them for YOU at YOUR DEMAND. Financially these facilities present a problem that can be solved only with the complete cooperation of the entire membership. YOU cannot logically demand certain facilities and leave it up to the BOARD OF TRUSTEES to pay for them. The congregation has a membership of approximately five hundred families. With such a roster the cost per member is inescapable. The amount is $74.40 per member per year.
>
> Examine the list carefully. You will note that it contains only those items that must be paid at regular intervals. It does not provide for essential miscellaneous items, for the retirement of principal obligations on mortgages, for a single delinquency in dues, for the payment of construction costs now past due, for the cost of auditorium seats and other bills that are clamoring for payment. You will note that the average cost per member per year for only those items on the list is far above the amount of dues established as a minimum. Therefore, some of us must pay more than others, according to our ability, to take care of the deficiency.

Isaac Shetzer became president of Shaarey Zedek in the dark and crucial days of 1932. A man of wisdom and courage, his statesman-like decisions gave strength to the congregation. Few loved the synagogue more, and none was more devoted to its welfare. With his limitless dedication and vigor, he set out to build the morale of the congregation. That he was successful is evident from the many new members who joined Shaarey Zedek within a short period of time.

Scores of prosperous Jewish merchants remembered the Isaac Shetzer who extended credit on the simple basis that most men were honest, who supplied them with a grubstake of a pack-full of dress lengths and notions when they first reached Detroit with no one to whom they could turn. They remembered the days of financial disaster when Isaac Shetzer devoted countless hours to helping them work out their financial difficulties. They remembered the man who intervened in behalf of many an embarrassed shopkeeper

List of Essential Expenditures

$24.00 per year per member for mortgage interest.

$15.00 per year per member for the Rabbi's salary.

$ 6.00 per year per member for the Cantor's salary.

$ 3.00 per year per member for the Sexton's salary.

$12.00 per year per member for janitor services, light, heat, water, janitor supplies, and building maintenance.

$10.60 per year per member for office supplies, stationery, telephone, postage, secretarial and bookkeeping services.

$ 3.80 per year per member for Sunday School salaries and upkeep.

$74.40 TOTAL PER YEAR PER MEMBER.

My father was interested in all those other activities, but the synagogue used to be his first love. My mother used to kid him about taking a cot down to the synagogue and sleeping there. My father worked very hard to get Consecration into Shaarey Zedek, and he and Harry Keidan led the first Consecration class down the aisle. I remember one letter from my father when I was away at college that was very exciting: "Today we laid the carpeting in the main sanctuary!" His letter was bursting with pride.

Miriam Shetzer Keidan

The Chicago Boulevard Synagogue Takes Shape

April 17, 1930: Excavations for the new building under way.

May 15, 1930: The basement is in; the forms are being laid in place for the steps of the main entrance.

June 12, 1930: The structural steel goes up for the main sanctuary.

July 10, 1930: Bricklayers at work on the skin of the building.

August 21, 1930: The exterior of the synagogue almost complete.

Looking down on the sanctuary from the balcony.

59

Procession of the Torah scrolls at the dedication of the Chicago Boulevard synagogue; leading the procession are Rabbi Abraham M. Hershman and Dr. Louis Finkelstein, The Jewish Theological Seminary of America.

PROGRAM

DEDICATION EXERCISES

CONGREGATION

SHAAREY ZEDEK

JANUARY 9 AND 10, 1932

SHEBAT, 1 AND 2, 5692

CHICAGO BOULEVARD AT LAWTON AVENUE

DETROIT

Program of the dedication exercises of Shaarey Zedek, January 9 and 10, 1932. The program began with the procession of the scrolls; the honors of opening and closing the ark were given to David Oppenheim and Isaac Shetzer. The key to the new synagogue was presented and accepted by Harry Z. Brown, chairman of the Building Committee and A. Louis Gordon, the congregational president; Abba Keidan lighted the perpetual light. Addresses were given by Dr. Leo M. Franklin, rabbi of Temple Beth El, and Dr. Louis Finkelstein, professor, The Jewish Theological Seminary of America; the dedication sermon was delivered by Rabbi Abraham M. Hershman.

Congregation Shaarey Zedek, Chicago Boulevard synagogue.

who was merely an account number in the ledgers of New York or Boston creditors — convincing those distant financiers that more could be accomplished by forbearance than by pressure.

Under Mr. Shetzer's leadership, the congregation looked forward to brighter days. The Friday evening services which had been so popular at Willis and Brush again became a regular part of the synagogue program. A class organized by Cantor Elias Zaludkowsky in which members could become familiar with the musical portions of the Friday evening services met every Monday night. In 1932, the Saturday evening songfests began. At Sabbath morning services, Rabbi Hershman would extend an invitation to these gatherings, and, under Cantor Zaludkowsky's guidance, the eighty to one hundred twenty participants would sing and sing and sing. When Cantor Zaludkowsky assumed another position, Cantor Jacob H. Sonenklar continued the songfests, which grew so large that the last one had to be held at the Statler Hotel. The congregation's interest in singing led to the addition of congregational singing to the regular synagogue service.

Abraham Satovsky was one of the Shaarey Zedek leaders who had begun his congregational activities as a youngster. He served as president of the Young People's Society, the Men's Club, and of the congregation and recalled with nostalgia coming in regularly from Ann Arbor, where he was a student at the University of Michigan, to distribute aliyahs to the young people of the Junior Congregation and to supervise their services when they were still at Willis and Brush. In the Chicago Boulevard synagogue, the Junior Congregation gained new vitality, sparked by the contributions of Joseph N. Keidan and Abraham Gordon. Abraham Gordon served for many years as its sponsor, and generations of Shaarey Zedek young people learned to love the synagogue and feel at home within its precincts thanks to his guidance and devotion. Shaarey Zedek was one of the first Conservative congregations in the United States to establish a Junior Congregation. Presidents or vice-presidents of the Junior Congregation who later served as leaders of Shaarey Zedek include among others Mandell L. Berman, Samuel Krohn, Harvey L. Weisberg, Leonard E. Baron, and Theodore Mandell.

The weekly congregational bulletin, the *Shaarey Zedek Recorder*, kept the membership informed on the activities of the various groups and encouraged greater interest in the synagogue. In 1933-34, the *Shaarey Zedek Yearbook* commented that "on Thursday mornings of each week, members of Congregation Shaarey Zedek have gotten into the habit of looking forward to receiving the paper which is now gaining favor as the organ of our synagogue."

Five hundred men and women filled the social hall to capacity on Sunday evening, December 25, 1932, in celebration of Chanukah, the seventieth anniversary of the congregation, and the twenty-fifth anniversary of Dr. Hershman's ministry at Shaarey Zedek. In recognition of Rabbi Hershman's many years of dedicated service, the congregation granted him a six-month leave of absence to travel in Palestine and Europe.

At this time, the congregation was experiencing severe financial difficulties. While it had to continue to meet its mortgage and operational obligations, the tenants of the building at Willis and Brush were unable to pay their rent. Heroic efforts were necessary to meet even partial payroll requirements. To raise funds, a Purim Subscription Dinner was scheduled for March 12, 1933, at the very substantial cost of fifteen dollars per couple. However, the bank holiday declared on February 14, 1933, necessitated a postponement. There could be no transactions involving checks, and there was not enough cash to finance the dinner. Following the reopening of the banks, the dinner was scheduled for May 14, 1933. Over one hundred fifty couples attended, and the congregation made a profit of $2,505.00

Negotiations with the contractors of the new building continued. The congregation was in no position to meet its full obligation and negotiated a settlement of fifty cents on the dollar.

News from Europe was of increasing concern to the Jewish community. Adolph Hitler became chancellor of the German Reich, and the Nazis relentlessly singled out the Jew for attack and

There was a time in Shaarey Zedek shortly after they moved to Chicago Boulevard when they used to have a Saturday night sing. It was open to the membership, and they would meet every Saturday night after services at some large home in the area. They sang with the cantor — about eighty to one hundred people came on a Saturday night. They would sing their heads off — sing Hebrew songs and then stop and drink gallons of coffee with great quantities of cake — and it was always announced in schule in whose house the sing would be. It was a wonderful activity.

Miriam Shetzer Keidan

Jess Milton Stein,
president of the Junior Congregation.

Arthur S. Purdy,
president of the Men's Club.

Mrs. Herbert H. Warner,
president of the Sisterhood.

Junior Congregation

It seems that the eternal problem of religion is youth. But there is no formidable antagonistic alignment of parent against child today. Modern youth is not so mad as to reject and deny those deeply-ingrained traditions wrought by the vigorous thinking of more than twenty hushed centuries.

The trouble is simply this: the world war, with all its repulsive brutality and lack of genuine idealism, has perverted the modern mind from its normal channels of wholesome thought to cynicism and disillusionment. And the new scientific method of research, the innumerable opportunities in music, literature, and government, have created such a multiplicity of interests that institutionalized religion is in danger of relegation to a rank of secondary importance.

By spreading a fresh spirit of hope and faith and by a greater aggressiveness of activity, the Junior Congregation believes it has succeeded in its aim — to revitalize the interest in Judaism.

Shaarey Zedek Yearbook, 1933-34

Men's Club of Shaarey Zedek

The aims of the Men's Club are to develop a close bond of interest among the members of Congregation Shaarey Zedek through social and recreational functions throughout the year; to foster through organized financial and personal support those activities which will strengthen the congregation and assist in its growth; to provide a forum for discussion of congregational affairs by its membership.

Our advocacy of the Friday night services, the Junior Congregation, and the *Recorder* have established them as Shaarey Zedek institutions. Social and educational features dot our calendar; a series of discussion of Jewish rituals, ceremonies, and traditions led by members of the community is being organized. It is our aim to emphasize our Judaism in all of our activities, to foster and develop a social life centering in the synagogue. Thus we feel we will contribute in the upbuilding of Shaarey Zedek as an institution that interests its membership throughout the year.

Shaarey Zedek Yearbook, 1933-34

Sisterhood of Shaarey Zedek

On the threshhold of a new year, the president of the Sisterhood of Congregation Shaarey Zedek extends hearty greetings for a blessed year to all its members, to the officers of the congregation, and also to the other affiliated organizations. Inspired by the holy day services — with renewed hope, courage, and faith, the Sisterhood pauses to contemplate as they rededicate themselves to the lofty ideals and noble aims of this organization, which are to strengthen traditional Judaism — by furthering the spiritual, material, and social interests of Congregation Shaarey Zedek — by advancing Jewish education among its members, by strengthening the Jewish institutions at home, and by generally strengthening the religious life of the local Jewish community.

Shaarey Zedek Yearbook, 1933-34

Leonard Sidlow,
president of the Young People's Society.

Young People's Society

The survival of any movement depends on a constant stimulus for youth. With this in mind, the Young People's Society is endeavoring to build a unit that will continually feed our senior societies with vitally interested new members. Beginning with the season of 1933-34, we are only extending the privilege of membership to individuals who will profess a definite interest in some phase of society work, namely, dramatics, study group, publication, music and choral, or any other activity for which there may be a great enough demand. For others, we are planning to provide open meetings of educational value, also recreational programs such as dances, movies, and teas.

Through this new plan we hope to awaken the young people at Shaarey Zedek to the responsibility of keeping the synagogue a vital institution, a place for cultural and social development as well as a place of worship.

Shaarey Zedek Yearbook, 1933-34

Jacob Keidan,
president of the Junior Young People's Society.

Junior Young People's Society

Founded in 1930 to afford social opportunities to sons and daughters of members of college age, the society plans several new undertakings this season. While in the past a large number of open meetings were held, this year the Board intends to hold as few as possible, for in the past the privileges accorded non-members too often meant that members had to meet the bills while others reaped the advantages. In addition, unwieldly groups hampered the fostering of friendships among the members and their personal participation in the society's activities. In the coming year, dramatics will be pushed extensively; there will be speakers of repute to discuss topics of immediate import to college-age men and women, and music, perhaps a society quartette, will be included; social gatherings, the largest part of the club's functions, will feature the traditional Woman's Dance for which invitations are issued by women members only, a summer formal dinner-dance at a country club, a Sunday afternoon dansant, and perhaps a repeat of the enormously successful Cabaret Dance of last year.

Shaarey Zedek Yearbook, 1933-34

Louis J. Gordon,
president of the Junior League.

Junior League of Shaarey Zedek

In order to satisfy the social aspirations of a number of young men and women who were not of age to join other Shaarey Zedek organizations, a new group was formed under the advisorship of Milton Marwil in 1933. The primary endeavor of the organization is to provide its members with short cultural programs followed by a social hour of dancing and light entertainment. The season was closed with a social affair at the New Whittier Hotel. Membership is open to those individuals between the ages of sixteen and eighteen whose parents are members of the synagogue and to a limited number of those whose parents are non-members. Like all new organizations the club has experienced its share of difficulties. However, the outlook for this season is bright.

Shaarey Zedek Yearbook, 1933-34

Hirsh B. Alper, sexton of Congregation Shaarey Zedek, 1920-1940. Revered for his kindness and piety, Mr. Alper conducted sessions in which the Talmud and Gemara were discussed after early morning services.

Dr. Hershman's message to the high school graduates of the Shaarey Zedek Religious School in 1932:

The following suggestive story is told in the Midrash. The famous Palestinian teacher, Rabbi Judah the Patriarch, on his return from a long journey, was visited by two of his disciples, Rabbi Jose and Rabbi Eleazar. He greeted them most cordially. "Draw nearer," he said to them. "I feel deeply indebted to you. It is you and your generation who will maintain Judaism after I and my contemporaries shall have gone the way of all flesh. You and your generation will owe a similar debt to your children and disciples; for otherwise what would become of Judaism!" "Consider Moses," he added. "Moses was the greatest teacher that the Jewish people has produced. Yet what would his teaching have been worth if those that came after him had not kept it up!" I would ask you, my young friends, to bear this great truth in mind. Cling to the synagogue. Attend its services. Continue your Jewish studies. Set a good example to your younger brothers and sisters. Exert your utmost effort to fulfill our expectations.

The Herald

stripped him of the rights of citizenship and the protection of the law. On March 29, 1933, many Shaarey Zedek members joined ten thousand Detroiters at a mass gathering at the Naval Armory to protest the German persecution of Jews and other minorities.

In 1933 Rabbi Hershman instituted an Adult Jewish School which offered courses in Hebrew, biblical studies, and history to the congregation, beginning a rich and varied program of adult education. Under the leadership of Arthur Purdy, the Men's Club was reorganized following the move to the new building at Chicago Boulevard, with dues set at two dollars a year. The program of 1933-34 included a social evening, a musical and dramatic evening, a symposium, a joint dinner meeting with the Men's Club of Temple Beth El, and a father and son program. Two years later the first Annual Forum took place, during the presidency of Harry M. Shulman. Speakers such as Oswald Harrison Villard and Dr. Shalom Spiegel established the tradition of bringing outstanding authorities and leaders before the congregation.

In December of 1934, Harry B. Keidan, chairman of the Education Committee, announced the formation of a congregational Hebrew school for members' children between the ages of six and ten, with a tuition fee of four dollars per month. In the same year Rabbi Hershman, who had been awarded the honorary degree of Doctor of Divinity in 1930, was awarded his second doctorate from The Jewish Theological Seminary of America, the degree of Doctor of Hebrew Literature, for his thesis on the history of the Jew of Spain and North Africa in the fourteenth and fifteenth centuries.

Some rays of light began to appear on the clouded horizon. The recently organized National Bank of Detroit assumed the obligations of the closed banks and gradually repaid their depositors. In 1935 the Detroit Savings Bank, holder of the mortgage on the building at Willis and Brush, received an offer from the Ebenezer A.M.E. Church to purchase the building for forty thousand dollars, and Shaarey Zedek turned the building over to the bank in return for a release from any further mortgage obligations.

Shaarey Zedek's library is now one of the finest American collections of Judaica associated with a synagogue, featuring Hebrew, English, and Yiddish books; periodicals; musical compositions and records; children's books; and an excellent file of educational material. It was formally inaugurated on December 16, 1935, endowed with ten thousand dollars by the Chevra Kadisha. Among the members who were most interested in its development were Isaac Saulson, Philip Rosenthal, Abe Caplan, David Zemon, Maurice Zackheim, and Ida Colten.

The Consecration service for girls was initiated in 1934. Mrs. Sol Kessler was instrumental in making it a beautiful and impressive occasion through which Jewish womanhood is approached with a sense of responsibility and dedication.

In an effort to recapture the spirit of Sabbath joy, the format of

EIGHT-DAY HOLIDAY FOR ALL BANKS IN MICHIGAN

DETROIT TIMES EXTRA

530 YEAR. NO. 137 · DETROIT, MICHIGAN, TUESDAY, FEBRUARY 14, 1933 · 24 PAGES · THREE CENTS

Proclamation Closing Banks to Protect State

Whereas, in view of the acute financial emergency now existing in the city of Detroit and throughout the state of Michigan, I deem it necessary in the public interest and for the preservation of the public peace, health and safety, and for the equal safeguarding without preference of the rights of all depositors in the banks and trust companies of this state and at the request of the Michigan Bankers' Association and the Detroit Clearing House and after consultation with the banking authorities, both national and state, with representatives of the United States Treasury Department, the Banking Department of the State of Michigan, the Federal Reserve Bank, the Reconstruction Finance Corporation, and with the United States Secretary of Commerce, I hereby proclaim the days from Tuesday, February 14th, 1933, to Tuesday, February 21st, 1933, both dates inclusive, to be public holidays during which time all banks, trust companies and other financial institutions conducting a banking or trust business within the state of Michigan shall not be opened for the transaction of banking or trust business, the same to be recognized, classed and treated and have the same effect in respect to such banks, trust companies and other financial institutions as other legal holidays under the laws of this state, provided that it shall not affect the making or execution of agreements or instruments in writing or interfere with judicial proceedings. Dated this 14th day of February, 1933, 1:32 a.m.
WILLIAM A. COMSTOCK, Governor of the State of Michigan.

ERNIE SCHAAF SUCCUMBS TO BRAIN OPERATION

STATEMENTS BY OFFICIALS

UNION GUARDIAN TRUST CO. DIFFICULTY CAUSES ORDER

During the Depression, I used to take my car downtown and park it for five cents all day. That's how bad things were. A haircut cost fifteen cents. The congregations couldn't pay salaries. One thing that stands to the credit of Shaarey Zedek is that every contractor who agreed to take fifty cents on the dollar was paid one hundred cents on the dollar. I remember being at a meeting when letters came from different contractors saying how very generous this was. When our building was first put up we had services in the social hall; the upstairs wasn't finished yet. Eventually we had enough money to continue building, but they had to eliminate a fancy social hall and gymnasium.

Robert Marwil

● THE MEN'S CLUB OF CONGREGATION

S H A A R E Y   Z E D E K

PROUDLY ANNOUNCES THE

F I R S T   A N N U A L

FORUM

Announcement of the First Annual Forum of the Men's Club, 1935-36, featuring Oswald Garrison Villard, editor of *The Nation*; Dr. Shalom Spiegel, professor of Hebrew Language and Literature at the Jewish Institute of Religion; Dr. Emil Lengyel, journalist and attorney, speaking on "The Boiling Cauldron of the Balkans"; Marvin Lowenthal, foreign correspondent; Dr. David de Sola Pool, rabbi of the Spanish-Portuguese Synagogue; Dr. Hans Kohn, lecturer on political science, Workmen's Seminary, Jerusalem; Rabbi Milton Steinberg, rabbi of the Park Avenue Synagogue.

Shaarey Zedek library.

67

First Consecration class of Congregation Shaarey Zedek, May 27, 1934.

1937 Consecration class.

I was active in the library, but we did not have any income. I also was president of the Chevra Kadisha. We saw that Mr. Lewis [who owned an undertaking establishment] started to make a lot of money from Shaarey Zedek, so we told him to give us ten percent of every funeral, and he consented. We collected ten thousand dollars that way, and with that money we filled the library with books. I was chairman of the library committee for over eight years, after David Zemon. It was running smoothly, but I must confess — my failure was that I loved Hebrew books, and whenever a new publication came out (I knew we didn't have money and but a few Hebrew book readers), I purchased the book.

Maurice H. Zackheim

the late Friday evening service was changed in 1934, replacing the formal program with community singing, musical selections by Cantor Sonenklar, brief talks by Rabbi Hershman, and refreshments in the social hall, giving a meaningful community emphasis to the concept of Oneg Shabbat cultivated in the Jewish home for generations.

The year 1937 marked the observance of the seventy-fifth anniversary of Shaarey Zedek. (Later studies of the history of Shaarey Zedek showed that it was established in 1861 rather than 1862; thus, 1936 was the true anniversary year.) The weekend of December 10 through December 12 was devoted to the anniversary celebration, which included speakers at Sabbath services, an anniversary dance, and a banquet on Sunday evening.

At a congregational meeting in September of 1937, it had been agreed to hire an assistant rabbi. On February 4, 1938, Morris Adler, rabbi of Temple Emanuel of Buffalo, New York, delivered an impressive sermon at the late Friday services, demonstrating his scholarship and his vital understanding of the problems which

Congregation Shaarey Zedek Religious School Honors Assembly, June 11, 1944.

Program of the seventy-fifth anniversary banquet of Congregation Shaarey Zedek, December 12, 1937. The toastmaster was Charles Rubiner; speakers were Maurice H. Zackheim, president of Shaarey Zedek; Rabbi Abraham M. Hershman; and Dr. Louis Finkelstein, The Jewish Theological Seminary of America. Mrs. Charles Robinson, president of the Sisterhood, presented a gift to the synagogue. Dinner music was provided by Michael Bistritsky, violinist; Harry Bistritsky, cellist; and Sam Solomon, cellist.

1862 · 1937

תרכ״ג — תרצ״ח

Seventy-fifth Anniversary
Congregation Shaarey Zedek

פתחו לי שערי צדק
"Open to me the Gates of Righteousness..."

Detroit, Michigan

Junior high school biblical history class taught by David Tanzman.

beset the modern Jew. The congregation invited Rabbi Adler to become its assistant rabbi, and he assumed his duties in September of that year.

Upon his arrival, Rabbi Adler immediately began to enlarge the mid-week school, to add to the requirements for Consecration, and to reorganize the Adult Institute. By 1960, he had helped to organize Conservative congregations in Michigan and had been identified with many civic and commercial projects. With the cooperation of several Shaarey Zedek members, he succeeded in increasing Shaarey Zedek's annual contribution to The Jewish Theological Seminary of America to the point that Shaarey Zedek led all other contributors for a number of years.

Rabbi Adler arrived in Detroit at a time of political and economic tension. The effects of the Depression were still in evidence — thirty thousand Detroit families were on welfare. On the political horizon, world Jewry faced signs of impending disaster. German troops had crossed the Austrian frontier and annexed Austria. The persecution of German Jews continued, and once again Shaarey Zedek members joined in a nationwide prayer of protest, on November 20, 1938.

Within this unsettling context, life at Shaarey Zedek went on much as usual. New activities were organized, such as a chess club and a fine orchestra led by Michael Bistritsky. The many new educational, cultural, and social activities of the congregation could not be housed in the existing facilities, and an adjoining building, the Kate Frank Memorial Building, was erected in 1939 to house classes and youth activities.

The world war which was to bring disaster to the world's largest and most dynamic Jewish community and tragedy to thousands of American families officially began on September 1, 1939, when Nazi troops invaded Poland. Two years later, on December 7, 1941,

Congregation Shaarey Zedek Honor Roll; those who died in World War I: Robert Blumberg, Mordecai Grossman, Lawrence Hertzberg, and Myron Rosenthal.

Shaarey Zedek Zionist meeting.

I feel that the greatest service which the Jewish Chaplain can render is to enable our young men to store up a harvest of pleasant experiences and associations with matters Jewish. My lads here drop in almost nightly to my office in the Chapel. They come to ask that I compose a Yiddish letter in their behalf, or for help in deciphering a letter that came form Bube. They bring to the Rabbi their perplexities and personal problems. They borrow magazines and books. They come to "requisition" a can of gefillte fish, stationery, or an air-mail stamp. They ask to hear the few Jewish records I have. The Chapel serves as the center around which much of the extramilitary life of our Jewish soldiers revolves. The services are completely theirs, for they come not as guests to a synagogue built for them by their elders, but as partners in a cooperative endeavor. Many come to "Shool" voluntarily for the first time in their lives.

The Chaplain here does not wish to, nor can he, withdraw to the Arctic climate of a remote, ivory tower. He shares fully in the life of his congregants; endures the same hardships; reacts to the same longings and needs; and knows their problems as only he can, who experiences them in his own life. Nor is the Chaplain permitted to retire to cloistered privacy once the services are concluded. The lads meet him in the "Chow-Line," at the movie, in the P-X, and under the shower. They know that he is a buddy, awaiting "rotation" and praying for his return home; "sweating it out" together with them. Every hard-working Chaplain has been rewarded with expressions such as "You are the first rabbi I ever spoke to, as man to man"; "Why was not Judaism presented in this way back home"; "I now have a better idea of how to bring up my child Jewishly."

From a letter written to congregation members by Rabbi Morris Adler from the Philippines; dated August, 1945

the United States entered the war, and 379 families of Shaarey Zedek sent husbands, fathers, and sons to defend the heritage of America.

During the war years, the membership of Shaarey Zedek subscribed over ten million dollars in war bonds. Among its members who served gallantly on the homefront was Perry Bernstein, one of the first doctors to offer his services to the Selective Service. Serving as examiner for Detroit's Draft Board No. 25, Dr. Bernstein developed medical implements to aid the rehabilitation of the wounded man and was commended by President Roosevelt for his outstanding contribution to the war effort.

The 40th Annual Convention of the Rabbinical Assembly was held at Shaarey Zedek on June 25, 1940, the first held in the Midwest. An Institute of Adult Jewish Studies affiliated with the National Academy for Adult Jewish Studies was organized in December of 1941. Led by Rabbis Hershman and Adler, the Institute offered courses in Hebrew language and literature, history, current events, and liturgy. A volume of outstanding biblical passages accompanied by Rabbi Adler's interpretation was published by the National Academy for Adult Jewish Studies in 1942 as *Great Passages from the Torah*.

The Holocaust intensified efforts to rebuild a Jewish homeland in Palestine. Shaarey Zedek, which had long been identified with the cause of Zionism, officially confirmed its support at an annual meeting held on April 28, 1943, urging its members to affiliate with Zionist organizations and pledge themselves to support to the utmost "the sacred project for the national restoration of Israel in the land of Israel."

On August 26, 1943, both the congregation and the community lost an outstanding leader with the death of Harry B. Keidan, who was equally devoted to Judaism and the American ideal. His private office had been a sanctuary where visitors were given not only advice but courage and strength with which to meet their problems. In the *Detroit Free Press*, he was described as the jurist par excellence: "Few men of our Bar and Bench have ever possessed so innately that capacity for impersonal judgment as did Judge Keidan. He was the blending of stern and inflexible justice with a compassionate pity for the wrongdoer . . . . The records will never show the long list of those who once stood before him to meet their fate, only to return later to be rehabilitated through the guidance of this great heart and mind."

In December of 1943 Rabbi Adler enlisted as a chaplain in the United States Army. Stationed first at the Rhodes General Hospital in Utica, he conducted services for patients and doctors, counseled the wounded and their parents, and published a periodical which carried inspirational messages. Goldie Adler organized classes for dependents of military personnel and was actively involved in Jewish community affairs. When Rabbi Adler was

Rabbi Morris Adler conducting Rosh Hashonah services in Yokohama, September, 1945, with Corporal Daniel Cohen of Brooklyn, N.Y. acting as cantor.

Program of the celebration of the burning of the mortgage on the Chicago Boulevard building, December 17, 1944.

PROGRAM

COMMEMORATING

BURNING OF THE MORTGAGE

OF

CONGREGATION SHAAREY ZEDEK

DETROIT - MICHIGAN

SUNDAY EVENING, DECEMBER 17, 1944

Program of
Mortgage Burning Ceremony

Opening Remarks	*Abraham Srere*
	Chairman of Evening
Readings from	
"The Maccabees"	*Dr. A. M. Hershman*
Mizmor Shir Chanukas	*Cantor Jacob H. Sonenklar*
	and String Quintette
Lighting of Candles and	
Hanaroz Halolu	*Cantor Sonenklar*
Address	*Dr. A. M. Hershman*
Ahl Hanissim and Ma-oz Tsur	*Cantor Sonenklar*
	and Congregation
Message from	
Rabbi Morris Adler	*President Harry Cohen*
Ceremony of Burning of	
Mortgage	*Isaac Shetzer, assisted by*
	Morris H. Blumberg
	Robert Marwil
	Maurice H. Zackheim
Address	*Dr. Louis Finkelstein, President of the*
	Jewish Theological Seminary of America
A-don Olam and	
America	*Cantor Sonenklar and Congregation*

•

HARRY M. SHULMAN, *General Chairman*

•

Following the Mortgage Burning Ceremonies,
the entire congregation is invited to the
Social Hall for an informal reception.

Page Three

Rabbi Abraham M. Hershman: 1907-1946, rabbi; 1946-1959, rabbi emeritus.

From time to time our home was the scene of a silent drama which epitomized Father's intense commitment to the tradition of Jewish learning. On those occasions when the desk in his study became too crowded for his needs, the dinner table was cleared after the evening meal, only to be set with a repast of quite another kind: a profusion of books of all sizes and descriptions, from thin volumes to heavy tomes, interlaced with innumerable sheets of paper inscribed with Hebrew and English notes. Father would sit at the table contentedly, immune to the sounds of the busy household around him, and absorb himself for hours on end in study and research — whether in preparation for a manuscript, or an address, or simply for his own edification.

Ruth and Eiga Hershman
in Michigan Jewish History, *June, 1981*

transferred to Japan, he was the first Jewish chaplain to be there after the American occupation and remained the only one for some time. With a Torah located in Australia and a shofar from the Philippines, he held religious services in a small Protestant chapel in Yokohama, and his chapel became a refuge for Jewish servicemen. A typical weekly schedule would find him conducting three services in Tokyo, two in Yokohama, six or seven on shipboard, and three in hospitals, as well as broadcasting over Radio Tokyo and writing one hundred or more letters to parents of soldiers in the area.

Fifteen hundred guests celebrated the burning of the Shaarey Zedek mortgage on December 17, 1944. Officiating were Dr. Louis Finkelstein, then president of The Jewish Theological Seminary of America, Rabbi Hershman, and Abraham Srere, a notable member of the congregation who had served Shaarey Zedek in many capacities over the years, including that of chairman of the Board of Trustees in 1925-26. President Harry Cohen read a message from Rabbi Adler. The honor of burning the mortgage was given to Isaac Shetzer, assisted by former presidents Morris H. Blumberg, Robert Marwil, and Maurice H. Zackheim.

The sanctuary was filled on May 13, 1945, as the congregation gathered to celebrate the Allied victory in Europe; on August 14, the war was over. But Rabbi Adler was still away in military service, and illness incapacitated Dr. Hershman. The Rabbinical Assembly had decided that a congregation might employ a temporary rabbi for the duration of the military service of its own rabbi, and in October of 1945, Rabbi Gershon Rosenstock joined the congregation; following Rabbi Adler's return to civilian life in 1946, Rabbi Rosenstock relinquished his position. It is interesting to note that 1945 marked the beginning of Hebrew instruction at Wayne State University, a program which eventually developed into the Department of Near Eastern Languages and Literatures.

The year of victory brought a loss to the congregation and to the community. Isaac Shetzer, who for more than four decades devoted a significant part of his life to Shaarey Zedek, died. It was his leadership which was responsible in large measure for the payment of over forty thousand dollars to contractors which he deemed a moral obligation, even though the congregation was not legally bound to make such payments. Fifteen hundred men and women from all walks of Jewish life attended the funeral services.

On October 14, 1946, the congregation accepted with deep regret the request of Rabbi Hershman to retire as rabbi of Shaarey Zedek. For his forty years of service, he was elected rabbi emeritus of the congregation and granted a pension. But Rabbi Hershman had retired only from the rabbinate; he continued his scholarship, immersing himself in his studies so deeply that his family would often have to remind him that it was time to eat or sleep. During this period, he wrote most of his published works. 1949 saw the

November 12, 1945

Officers and Board of Trustees of Congregation Shaarey Zedek

offer the following

Resolution

With deepest sorrow and regret, we record the death of

⤳ Isaac Shetzer ⤳

While his passing leaves a mournful void in the entire community of Detroit, this Congregation suffers a special loss in the death of this good and gifted servant, so much of whose time, energy and spirit were devoted to its welfare.

From his earliest manhood he sensed in an extraordinary degree, the vital place that the synagogue and the religious school occupied in the life of the Jew, and, with all the conviction of his own sterling character, he constantly inspired others to share with him the joy and delight, which were his in laboring in the vineyard of his people.

Possessed of a love, and understanding, of the precious truths of Judaism; of an indomitable will for its preservation; of a zeal for the living out of his faith that rose above all obstacles of time and place; of wisdom in counsel and courage in action, it was inevitable that there should be conferred upon him the highest official honors in the gift of the Congregation which he served so faithfully, and so well, for many long years.

Nor was he content to express himself only in service to the synagogue. Every facet of Jewish life had some claim upon his interest. As founder of the Chebra Kadisha of Congregation Shaarey Zedek, as president of the Hebrew Free Loan Association, as one who took an important part in the organization of the Clover Hill Park Cemetery, as a leader in all Zionist activities, as a member of the Board of Governors of the Jewish Welfare Federation, and as a participant in many other social and philanthropic movements, he was a tower of strength for all to draw upon.

Be it therefore Resolved, by the Board of Trustees of Congregation Shaarey Zedek, that the sentiments herein expressed be recorded in the permanent records of the Congregation, and that there be extended to his family, in their bereavement, the heartfelt sympathy of the Congregation and of all of its members.

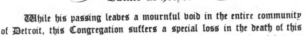

PRESIDENT

VICE-PRESIDENT

TREASURER

SECRETARY

Resolution recording the death of Isaac Shetzer, expressing the sympathy of the congregation to his family; dated November 12, 1945, and signed by Rabbis Hershman and Adler and the officers and Board of Trustees of Congregation Shaarey Zedek.

1947 Consecration class.

publication by the Yale University Press of Dr. Hershman's study of the Book of Judges of the Code of Maimonides as the third volume in its Judaica series. Dr. Hershman had devoted years of study and research to the preparation of this carefully edited text of the fourteenth book of Maimonides' Code, adding an introduction based on original manuscripts to his translation.

Rabbi Hershman pursued his hobbies with the same logic and absorption. During his college and seminary days, he had become so enamored of chess that, as he often told, he once devoted an entire summer to it, sitting in a chess club morning, noon, and night. He finally wrenched himself away in self-defense, but he never really lost interest, and whenever he could find time and a ready partner, he would sit down and lose himself in a game of chess. Baseball, too, never failed to be a source of amusement. Again, in his careful, rational manner, Rabbi Hershman became an armchair strategist — excited at a crucial point, but always the logician, learning the batting averages of the players, their strengths and weaknesses, and criticizing and correcting the strategy of the team managers.

On October 24, 1946, Shaarey Zedek unanimously elected Morris Adler rabbi of the congregation.

The war was over, and many of the Jewish young men who returned to civilian life came to the doors of Shaarey Zedek. A year's free membership was extended to each. Before long, it was obvious that the Jewish population was again moving north; an increasing number of members lived a good distance from the synagogue building, and children and their parents were spending too

Religious school class.

Janet Olender, Shaarey Zedek librarian *(second from the left),* accepts a citation of merit on behalf of Congregation Shaarey Zedek from Rabbi I. Edward Kiev at the annual meeting of the Jewish Book Council of America, held on May 19, 1948, at the Jewish Welfare Board, New York City.

much time driving to and from the synagogue for school and extra-curricular activities. At a meeting of the congregation on October 14, 1947, President Harry M. Shulman announced that a committee had been appointed to investigate the possibility of erecting a youth and school building in a suitable location.

The congregation continued to inaugurate new programs and activities. Rabbi Adler, Leonard Sidlow, Hyman Safran, and Milton M. Maddin visited congregational nursery schools in regard to the establishment of a nursery school at Shaarey Zedek. The complexities of a large congregation prompted Shaarey Zedek to invite Joseph Abrahams to assume the post of executive director. During the same year, the Sisterhood was able to establish a Jewish Theological Seminary of America scholarship in honor of Rabbis Hershman and Adler.

Shaarey Zedek nursery school youngsters celebrate Purim with Rabbi Morris Adler.

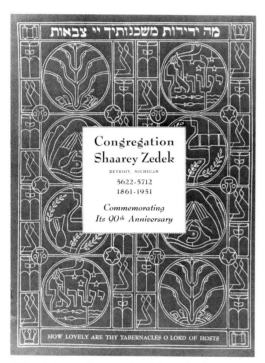

Ninetieth anniversary booklet, which included a short history of the congregation.

By March of 1948 the Education Committee reported plans to establish a nursery class to meet five mornings a week, accommodating not more than thirty children. Ninety applications poured in within weeks of the announcement. One year after the Beth Hayeled nursery school began operations in September of 1948, a kindergarten was established to provide a continuity of educational experience. In September of 1950 a program of instruction was offered to the six-year-old graduates of the daily kindergarten class. Meeting twice during the week and on Sunday morning the Mechinah program was the forerunner of the educational program later instituted for all six-year-olds.

In honor of its ninetieth anniversary, celebrated during the Thanksgiving week of 1951, Shaarey Zedek published a brief history of the congregation and sponsored an exhibit at The Detroit Institute of Arts of Jewish ceremonial art lent in the main by The Jewish Museum of The Jewish Theological Seminary of America and Shaarey Zedek's Charles Feinberg. Dr. Stephen Kayser, curator of The Jewish Museum, delivered a lecture on Jewish ceremonial art. The anniversary was further marked by addresses, programs, and an anniversary banquet.

The Board considered a number of sites for a branch building for school and youth activities. In May of 1952, a lot was purchased at the corner of West Seven Mile Road and Lesure, and Alex Kohner was engaged as the architect. Charles Rubiner, who became president of Shaarey Zedek in 1950, wrote in a message to the congregation: "The ninety years of Shaarey Zedek's history are dotted with the periodic wanderings of its members away from the synagogue's neighborhood. . . . No one is suggesting that the Shaarey Zedek synagogue move to a new site, nor is that thought within contemplation at present. Our educational facilities are, however, more

Mrs. Sidney Winer, Mrs. Kolman Sachse, Daniel C. Cullen, Mrs. Alex Wilenkin, Mrs. Ben Jaffe, Mrs. Joseph Orley, and Mrs. Samson Wittenberg rehearse for a performance of the cantata, "The Lord's Song," presented in celebration of the congregation's ninetieth anniversary on November 24, 1951.

1953 Consecration class.

Exhibition of Jewish Ceremonial Art, The Detroit Institute of Arts, November 15—December 30, 1951

Congregation Shaarey Zedek, now marking the ninetieth anniversary of its founding, has arranged for this exhibition in fulfillment of its profound interest in this significant aspect of the religious life and as its contribution to the cultural life of Detroit. May this exhibit contribute to a deepening of the appreciation of the sanctity and beauty of the tradition it represents. May it stimulate the religious life of our great city to render the holy, beautiful and the beautiful, holy.

Rabbi Morris Adler

Mrs. William Appel and her children Avram and Mary read a parchment Torah from the exhibit of Jewish ceremonial art held at The Detroit Institute of Arts from November 15 to December 30, 1951.

Pair of Torah headpieces (rimonim), silver and gilt; German (Frankfort-am-Main), c. 1705; Master: Jeremias Zobel; The Jewish Museum. Rimonim (pomegranates), together with bells, refer to the garment of the biblical high priest: "A golden bell and a pomegranate, upon the skirts of the robe round about (Ex. 28:34).

Wedding ring in the form of a synagogue, silver; Austrian (Eisenstadt), 1690; formerly collection Charles E. Feinberg. Inscribed in Hebrew with the name of the owner, Samson Wertheimer, and of Rabbi Meir ben Isaac, who performed the wedding ceremony. Samson Wertheimer was the famous Austrian court Jew; the wealthiest Jew of his day, from 1694 to 1709 Wertheimer was the chief financial administrator of the emperors Leopold I, Joseph I, and Charles VI, placing enormous sums at the disposal of the government during the Spanish War of Succession and the war against Turkey and acting as a diplomatic agent as well.

Rabbi Morris Adler is pictured with Walter
Reuther *(fifth from the left)* in his effort to get
the unions involved in buying Israel Bonds. A
friend of Walter Reuther, Rabbi Adler served
as chairman of the Public Review Board of the
United Auto Workers from 1957-1966.

Hyman Safran, who became president of
Shaarey Zedek in 1956, holds the Torah
scrolls; *left:* Jacob A. Epel, a fine Jewish scholar
who became sexton in 1940.

The Daily Minyan
In all the decades of Shaarey Zedek's history, a
group of men assembled every morning and
every evening to participate in daily worship.
Some attend to recite kaddish, others to celebrate a joyous event, and yet others because
the words of the service are woven into the
experience of each day. Grief, joy, pain, and
laughter are shared by this select group in the
ongoing and regular encounter with the presence of God and with each other. In the daily
minyan, the synagogue is experienced as a
place of comfort, friendship, and spiritual comfort.

directly affected. Hundreds of our children are now obliged to spend a substantial part of the limited time available for religious instruction in traveling to and from our present school." Pending the construction of the branch building, arrangements were made in 1952 for the use of classrooms at the MacDowell school. For the growth and contribution of the religious school to Jewish education, the congregation was awarded the Solomon Schechter Award by the United Synagogue of America for 1952-53. During that period Eliot S. Schwartz was educational director and Leonard Sidlow chairman of the Education Committee.

The Joint Adult Institute, sponsored by the Conservative congregations of Detroit, was organized in 1952. Congregations Adas Shalom, Ahavas Achim, Beth Aaron, and B'nai Moshe joined Shaarey Zedek in presenting a series of twenty Tuesday evenings in which the rabbis served as instructors, assisted by a number of outstanding visiting lecturers and scholars.

Groundbreaking ceremonies for the branch building took place on Sunday, March 8, 1953. October 25 marked the dedication of the spacious building with seven well-equipped classrooms, an arts and crafts room, and a suite of offices which provided educational facilities for Beth Hayeled and elementary school classes for many years.

Although Shaarey Zedek was by no means ready to make another move, the Capital Planning Committee had been studying population trends and examining sites for a future home. At a special meeting of the congregation on January 14, 1954, the members present unanimously approved the purchase of a fifteen-acre tract of land on Northwestern Highway and 10½ Mile Road.

A number of honors were bestowed on Rabbi Adler in 1954, recognizing his scholarship and his role as a leader in the congregation and the community. After fifteen years as Shaarey Zedek's rabbi, he was given lifetime tenure, and he was hailed as a spiritual leader of the community whose voice carried far beyond the boundaries of his own faith at a dinner given for him at the St. Cyprian's Episcopal Church. In November Dr. Louis Finkelstein announced the appointment of Rabbi Adler as visiting professor of Homiletics at The Jewish Theological Seminary of America for the spring semester of 1955; Rabbi Adler was to begin teaching after he returned from a visit to Israel.

It was now evident that the congregation, which had grown to fifteen-hundred members, required the services of an assistant rabbi, and Rabbi Milton Arm was invited to join the synagogue staff. He remained until 1958, when he resigned to accept a position with another congregation.

The Shaarey Zedek Kibbutz

In the 1950s a congregational fellowship of men established the annual Kibbutz, held at Leonard Sidlow's summer home near Traverse City. The men would gather for five days in spring for study, discussion, worship, and camaraderie, led by Rabbi Adler and occasional guest lecturers. The Kibbutz informally held a formal dinner on the last evening of the retreat. One of the groups solemnized their dinner with their signatures on a place mat.

First row (seated and kneeling, left to right): Max Borin, Louis Galen, Ira Kaufman, Bert Smokler, Abe Katzman, Leo Weiner, Ben Good, Oscar Kramer, Ben Chinitz, Leonard Sidlow; *second row (standing, left to right):* Albert Altman, Sam Firestone, Rabbi Adler, Henry Berris, Ben S. Sidlow, Daniel C. Cullen, Dan Mendelson, Cantor Sonenklar, Bud Marwil.

In 1954, the Junior Congregation held its first yearly Kibbutz Koton at Camp Tamarack in May. Twenty-nine youngsters, accompanied by ten adult sponsors, spent a weekend in intensive study, prayer, services, and cultural and social activities patterned after the annual five-day adult Kibbutz organized in 1948. The annual reunion of Shaarey Zedek alumni at the University of Michigan at Ann Arbor was also initiated.

The American Jewish community commemorated the three-hundredth anniversary of Jewish settlement in the United States in 1954, and Shaarey Zedek joined congregations throughout the country in ceremonies held in September to offer thanks for the blessings of America.

The congregation was growing larger and younger. In 1955, it was obvious that within a year the number of thirteen-year-old boys would exceed the number of Sabbaths, so it was decided that there might be two Bar Mitzvahs on a Sabbath. For Shaarey Zedek youngsters between the ages of five and ten, a summer day camp accommodating one hundred thirty was established with Samuel Milan as director. Wilbur S. Stein accepted the post of executive director of Shaarey Zedek and quickly assumed the ever-increasing responsibilities of this vital administrative position.

Cantor Reuven Frankel became the chazzan sheni of the congregation in 1956. He had served as cantor of Congregation Sons of Israel of Asbury Park, New Jersey, and Congregation B'nai Zion of Chattanooga, Tennessee. Eli Grad was invited to become the educational director in the same year. A graduate of The Jewish Theological Seminary of America and New York University, Mr. Grad brought to his new position a rich and varied background in the administration of religious schools from his previous position as principal of the B'nai Israel Congregational School of Washington, D.C. In 1956 two talented educators joined the Beth Hayeled staff: Jessica Zimmerman as director and Rosaline Gilson as a teacher;

First Shaarey Zedek braille class, 1955-56: Mrs. Morris Adler, Mrs. Sidney Cohen, Mrs. Joseph Edelman, Mrs. Perry Goldman, Mrs. Nathan Milstein, Mrs. Norman Noble, Mrs. Abraham Shoyer, Mrs. David Steinman, Mrs. Sam Wasserman, and Mrs. Max Yorke with their teacher, Miss Ella McLennan. The eighteen-week class was arduous, and the Library of Congress allowed only five mistakes in each book transcribed into braille.

Shaarey Zedek Bar Mitzvah boys.

Shaarey Zedek choral group; *first and third from the right:* Cantor Reuven Frankel and Cantor Jacob H. Sonenklar.

Israel Bond Drive, 1956; *left to right:* Mrs. Morris Adler; Mrs. Baer Keidan, president of the Sisterhood; Mrs. Charles Milan; Mrs. Eleanor Roosevelt; Mrs. Leonard Sidlow; Mrs. Hyman Safran; Mrs. Abraham Satovsky.

At a Chanukah dinner in 1955, a portrait of Rabbi Abraham M. Hershman was unveiled; Rabbi and Mrs. Morris Adler, Rabbi Hershman, and Dr. and Mrs. Leonard Sidlow were photographed at the head table.

since 1968 Mrs. Gilson has been the director of the Beth Hayeled and has supervised the school's growth from 96 to 206 children.

To evaluate the congregation's tract of land on Northwestern Highway and 10½ Mile Road as a site for a new synagogue, the Board retained Percival Goodman, a well-known architect who had designed over thirty synagogue buildings and won many awards for his designs. Based on studies of the future needs of the congregation, Mr. Goodman found the tract too small; the land was later sold to the Burroughs Corporation. At a special meeting held on February 28, 1957, Shaarey Zedek members approved the purchase of a forty-acre site on Northwestern Highway and Eleven Mile Road. Mr. Goodman and the firm of Albert Kahn Associates were hired to design the new synagogue.

The fifty-year anniversary of Rabbi Hershman's first days at Shaarey Zedek was celebrated on November 6, 1957. As a tribute to his lifelong dedication to Zionism and his efforts on behalf of the State of Israel, the celebration also marked the conclusion of the year's fundraising on behalf of State of Israel bonds. In honor of

Rabbi Hershman, the students of the Shaarey Zedek religious schools began the planting of a forest of ten thousand trees in Israel.

The first of a series of Hebrew adaptations of Broadway musicals was presented at the Youth Awards Night sponsored by the Men's Club on April 2, 1958. Shaarey Zedek young people, under the direction of Helen Shur and Janet Pont, staged "Oklahoma," for which they prepared the Hebrew translation.

Cantor Jacob H. Sonenklar's twenty-five years of dedicated service were honored at a Silver Anniversary Dinner on June 8, where he was presented with a trip to Israel in recognition of his outstanding service. Louis Berry was elected president in 1958. One of the community's most devoted workers, he received the Louis Marshall Award of The Jewish Theological Seminary of America in the same year.

In 1958 the B'nai Brith Hillel Foundation published Rabbi Adler's *The World of the Talmud.* Written primarily for college students, it provides a lucid glance at the Talmud valuable to every Jewish reader. Wayne State University awarded Rabbi Adler an honorary doctorate in 1960; the citation mentioned his scholarship, his many services to the community, and his wide range of humanitarian interests.

Jacob H. Sonenklar, cantor of Congregation Shaarey Zedek, 1932-1969; cantor emeritus 1969-.

The Congregation Assembled for Prayer in the Chicago Boulevard and Southfield Sanctuaries

And Jacob said: How awesome is this place, it is the very House of God. We, the people of this congregation, do now rededicate ourselves to the worship of God in this place so that we may help the establishment of His Kingdom on earth.

We resolve that this synagogue will enable us to know the profound wisdom of our ancient tradition and the highest expression of the modern spirit. We remember Sabbaths and holy days; days of Bar Mitzvah and Bat Mitzvah, days of Consecration and graduation, and the days of the joining together of husband and wife in hallowed love.

The Recorder

III. Southfield
1961-1981

At the 100th annual meeting of the congregation on April 12, 1961, which was also the best-attended meeting of the century, over seven hundred members approved the recommendation of the Board of Directors to build a new synagogue on the forty-acre site in Southfield Township. From the very beginning, Shaarey Zedek members had been actively involved in determining the needs of the congregation.

The standing committees of the synagogue had been expanded to commissions, and all members of the congregation had been urged to join the commission of their choice to help in programming the proposed building. Hence, the combined work of several hundred members went into the two volumes of drawings and specifications presented to the synagogue in December of 1960. The new facilities planned for a growing congregation included a main sanctuary of twelve hundred seats which could be expanded through the use of movable walls to include the social halls on either side, providing an area which could seat thirty-six hundred on the High Holy Days. The entire membership of seventeen hundred families would now be able to sit together for the first time in many years. The Adult Chapel would serve smaller gatherings. For the Shaarey Zedek children, there were to be facilities for a youth lounge, auditorium, and chapel in addition to extensive classrooms. A spacious library was planned, a kitchen which could serve over six hundred fifty persons, and the necessary meeting rooms and administrative offices.

Bids on these plans were submitted by seven prime contractors. The cost for the entire project — including land, architectural fees, landscaping, and furnishings — was estimated at $4,800,000, almost one million dollars over the estimates projected by the architects the year before. Many members of the congregation at the decisive meeting of April 12, 1961, expressed their hearty concern over what seemed at that time to be an extraordinary amount of money. Could the congregation support an endeavor of that dimension? Should the congregation build in the suburbs when the present synagogue was not only adequate but also stood as an affirmation of the congregation's commitment to the city of Detroit? The spirited discussion continued with the members frankly presenting their views in the best tradition of a town meeting. There were voices that counseled patience, arguing for a postponement that would permit further review. Rabbi Adler made an eloquent plea for immediate endorsement of the plans, picturing the spiritual, educational, and social needs that could be met in the proposed building. And, finally, when Hyman Safran offered the motion to accept the proposal to build, the vote to approve was overwhelming.

On a windy spring Sunday, May 28, 1961, more than a thousand members drove out into the middle of what then seemed to be nowhere to participate in groundbreaking ceremonies. Several

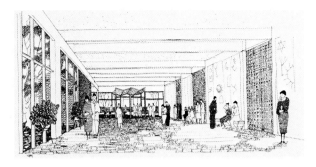

Sketches from the designs of Percival Goodman for the main lobby and the children's library.

The Commissions Begin Their Work for the New Synagogue

The Building Commission. *Seated (left to right):* Gilbert B. Silverman, Charles N. Agree, Mandell L. Berman; *standing:* Abraham Satovsky, Wilbur S. Stein, Maurice S. Schiller (Hyman Safran is absent).

The House Commission. *Seated (left to right):* Manuel Zechman, Arthur Fleischman, Gilbert B. Silverman, Phillip Zimmerman, Morris Gross; *standing:* Hyman A. Keidan, Wilbur S. Stein, Louis R. Gelfand, Jay M. Rosenthal.

The Youth Commission. *Left to right:* Louis E. Heideman, Elaine Krohn, Leonard Antel, Jay M. Rosenthal, Wilbur S. Stein, Abe Katzman, Leo Weiner, Florence Friedman, Mel Katz, Frank Rosenbaum, Leah Katz.

The Education Commission. *First row (left to right):* Jay M. Rosenthal, Eli Grad, Phillip Zimmerman, Florence Friedman, Elaine Krohn, Samuel Krohn, Leo Weiner, Frank Rosenbaum, Abe Katzman; *second row (left to right):* Jessica Zimmerman, Daniel C. Cullen, Marion Shulevitz, Harry Balberor, Ruth Appel, Louis E. Heideman, Wilbur S. Stein, Alex Zuckman.

ORDER OF SERVICE

Presiding: MANDELL BERMAN, Chairman, Building Committee

PRESENTATION OF COLORS . . Sholom Post, Jewish War Veterans

NATIONAL ANTHEM . . . . . Led by Cantor Jacob H. Sonenklar

INVOCATION . . . . Rabbi Irwin Groner

RESPONSIVE READING . . . . Dr. Leonard Sidlow
   (See opposite page)   Chairman, Ground Breaking Ceremony

HYMN . . . . Religious School Choirs led by Cantor Reuven Frankel

GREETINGS

HON. JAMES CLARKSON, Mayor of Southfield
HAYIM DONIN, Rabbi, B'nai David Synagogue, Southfield
ABRAHAM SATOVSKY, President of the Congregation
LOUIS BERRY, Chairman, Building Fund Campaign

TURNING OF THE SOD CEREMONIES

50-YEAR MEMBERS

5th GENERATION MEMBERS

PRESIDENTS OF AFFILIATED ORGANIZATIONS

ADDRESS . . . . Rabbi Morris Adler

BENEDICTION . . . . Rabbi Irwin Groner

"ADON OLOM" . . . . Congregation

GROUND BREAKING CEREMONIES

marking the start of construction of our new

CONGREGATION
SHAAREY ZEDEK
SYNAGOGUE

Sunday, May 28, 1961 — 11 a. m.

JAMES COUZENS AT 11½ MILE ROAD

The youngest generation, together with the senior generation, cuts the ribbon.

generations of Shaarey Zedek families watched Andy Schiller, Bruce Keidan, Sara Keidan, Andrea Fleischman, and Sandy Berris, representatives of the fifth generation of Shaarey Zedek, cut the symbolic ribbon to begin the ceremonies. The centennial dinner that evening was highlighted by Dora Erlich's recollections of her girlhood days at Shaarey Zedek under the tutelage of Rabbi Hershman. Louis C. Miriani, then mayor of Detroit, declared May 28 Congregation Shaarey Zedek Day. Centennial events continued on through 1961; one thousand members attended the synagogue's Chanukah Ball at Cobo Hall, where Rabbi Adler spoke of the congregation's splendid past and of his faith in its future in its handsome new building.

A little more than a year later, on December 15, 1962, the congregation held its last service in the sanctuary on Chicago Boulevard. The last issue of the *Recorder* to come from that building recalled the thirty years there as years of progress and growth from a few hundred members to over seventeen hundred, from a handful of students in the Hebrew school to well over one thousand. It was time to move on.

In his dedicatory sermon at the first Havdalah service in the new building, Rabbi Adler told the congregation to direct its thoughts

Fifty-year members of the synagogue turn the first spades-full of dirt for the new synagogue, Sunday, May 28, 1961: Julius Steinberg, Maurice H. Zackheim, Abraham Srere, Louis J. Rosenberg, Julius Berman, Harry Cohen, Hyman A. Keidan, Max Krell.

COMMON COUNCIL OF THE CITY OF DETROIT
Resolution.

TESTIMONIAL TO CONGREGATION SHAAREY ZEDEK

WHEREAS, Congregation Shaarey Zedek is presently observing the centennial of its founding, and

WHEREAS, Since 1861, Shaarey Zedek has continuously served as a House of prayer, study and dedication, inspiring many generations of men and women to lives of service, faith and righteousness, and

WHEREAS, Its members have been among the honorable, constructive and devoted citizens, contributing to the development of the religious, economic, social, academic, civic areas of our common life, and

WHEREAS, There have come from Congregation Shaarey Zedek men of vision and dedication who gave leadership to philanthropic, educational and political endeavors, having for their purpose the enhancement of the many-faceted life of Detroit, and

WHEREAS, Its late president, Mr. David W. Simons, was one of Detroit's most distinguished citizens serving as a member of the first nine-man Common Council, and

WHEREAS, Its spiritual leaders have been and are men of learning and character whose teachings and counsel have helped enrich the spiritual life of our community, and have advanced the cause of freedom, brotherhood and justice in our midst, NOW, THEREFORE, BE IT

RESOLVED, That we express our deep appreciation to Congregation Shaarey Zedek for its record of a hundred years of service to God and man; and wish that it may continue to serve as a citadel of faith and a lighthouse of inspiration, and thus contribute to the welfare, life and spiritual quality of all the citizens of our great city.

ADOPTED May 23, 1961

Mary V. Beck
President, Common Council

Ed. Carey

Edward Connor

William T. Patrick Jr.

Don D. Rogell

Thomas D. Leadbetter
City Clerk

Del A. Smith

Eugene Van Antwerp

Blanche Parent Wise

Charles V. Youngblood

Chas. Williams
City Treasurer

Louis C. Miriani
Mayor

The Detroit Common Council takes note of the 100th anniversary of the synagogue and remembers that David W. Simons, one-time president of Shaarey Zedek, was also a member of Detroit's first Common Council.

You and your Family are invited to attend the

Chanukah Dinner and Ball

Celebrating the 100th Anniversary Year of

Congregation Shaarey Zedek

on Sunday, the third of December

Cobo Hall

Address by

Dr. Louis Finkelstein
Chancellor
Jewish Theological Seminary of America

Music by the Felix Resnick Orchestra

Champagne at 6:00
Dinner at 6:30
Dress Optional

Please respond before
Monday, November 27th
$8.00 per person

Festivities in celebration of Shaarey Zedek's 100th birthday continued throughout the anniversary year.

5621	1861
5721	1961

You and your family
are invited to attend the

CENTENNIAL DINNER

Inaugurating the
100 Anniversary Year of

CONGREGATION
SHAAREY ZEDEK

Sunday, May twenty-eighth
in the Social Hall

Champagne at 6:30
Dinner following
Dress optional

Please respond
$8.00 per Person

Charles Rubiner presents a citation to Philip Slomovitz, editor of *The Detroit Jewish News*, at the Centennial Chanukah Ball.

The inauguration of the 100th anniversary year of the congregation celebrated in the social hall the evening of the groundbreaking ceremony. Rabbi Irwin Groner and Cantor Jacob H. Sonenklar officiate at the cutting of the bread and the recital of "ha-motzi."

Under Construction

The main sanctuary is flanked by two equilateral triangles, the social halls, which can be joined to the sanctuary to form one great seating area for the High Holy Days. A smaller chapel, seating 250 people, carries out the same motifs as the larger on a reduced scale. The lobby, 100 feet in length and 36 feet wide, connects the two sanctuaries. Two corridors lead to the administrative complex and the classrooms. A lower level houses youth activities and provides for an auditorium or chapel. Architects were Percival Goodman of New York and Albert Kahn Associated Architects and Engineers of Detroit. O. W. Burke Company was general contractor.

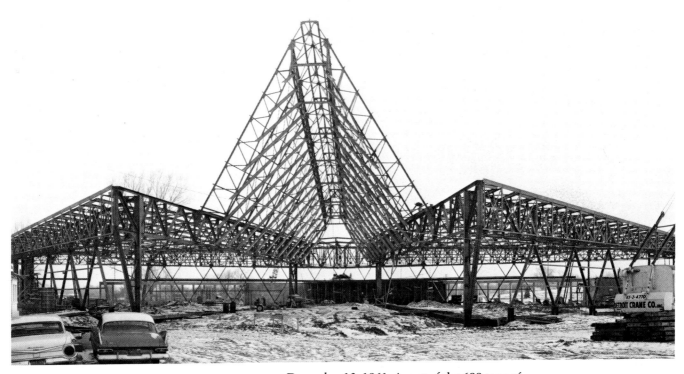

December 13, 1961: A part of the 600 tons of structural steel required for the building complex rises to form the main sanctuary and the adjacent wings.

August 8, 1962: The great roof is pitched over the area to contain the ark, still swathed in the wooden forms to hold the poured concrete.

October 5, 1962: The entrance to the main sanctuary is framed by precast concrete elements. 20,000 square feet of plate glass and 14,400 square feet of precast concrete panels will be used in the completed building.

December 3, 1962: Inside the sanctuary, the sun pours through the openings that will carry the stained glass windows.

Laying the Cornerstone for the New Synagogue: June 17, 1962

Over two thousand members attended the ceremonies in the unfinished social hall. Rabbis Adler and Groner, Cantors Sonenklar and Frankel, and the present and past officers of the congregation participated in a processional to the cornerstone, located at the entrance to the new building. Rabbi Adler asked each participant to place one item in the cornerstone. Sealed in the stone were records removed from the cornerstones of the buildings at Winder Street, Willis and Brush, and Chicago Boulevard; a letter to the future; some fifty-four hundred names inscribed by Shaarey Zedek on parchment cards; a brief history of Shaarey Zedek published on its ninetieth anniversary; a set of United States coins minted in 1962 together with a set of Israeli coins, symbolizing the kinship of the people of Israel with the land of Israel; copies of the *Detroit Jewish Chronicle, The Detroit News,* and the *Detroit Free Press,* and other records and mementoes of Shaarey Zedek.

Louis Berry, chairman of the Development Fund, David M. Miro, president of the synagogue, and Mandell L. Berman, chairman of the Building Committee, assist Rabbi Morris Adler with the transference of the contents of the cornerstone from the old synagogue.

Mayor James Clarkson of Southfield, Michigan, offers his congratulations to the congregation at the cornerstone ceremonies. *To his left:* President David M. Miro, Louis Berry, Max M. Fisher, Cantor Jacob H. Sonenklar, Samuel Krohn, Mandell L. Berman, Cantor Reuven Frankel.

Parents, children and grandparents of the 1,700-family congregation sat on wobbly chairs on sand, on planks, on a partly finished concrete dividing wall, or just stood, as they unburdened the joy of their hearts and looked to the future. Randy David Slomovitz, 5½, built what he called a "castle" in the sand as his grandfather listened attentively to Rabbi Morris Adler call for "imagination." Rabbi Adler said children there that day would look back 50 or 60 years and remember proudly they were at the first ceremony in the new building. "We're building here for centuries," he said.

The Detroit Free Press, June 18, 1962

105

The Meaning of the Synagogue

The main sanctuary is built upon the geometric form of the triangle, symbolic of Mt. Sinai, as is the craggy, rough-hewn exterior. But the triangle which dominates the main sanctuary and the small chapel that faces the inner court also represents the elements which form the Star of David, as well as the two hands joined in prayer. The ten projections on the soaring facade signify the Ten Commandments. The sanctuary is oriented on the ark, formed of Israeli marble in dramatic contrast to the elaborate stained glass windows that frame it. Split in the center, the ark is an echo of the two tablets brought down from the Mount. The ner tomid created in stainless steel by Jan Peter Stern represents the tree of life, the burning bush, and culminates in a menorah-like shape.

Robert Pinart's stained glass windows again present the burning bush out of which God spoke to Moses. Yellow and brown for the trees and vegetation are gradually dominated by the more brilliant hues of the flame. The framing of the ark in black and raw wood is deliberate in its unfinished appearance, for there is a Jewish custom not to complete a building in mourning for the loss of Zion. The effect of ribbing along the walls suggests the tent of meeting used by the Jews in their exodus from Egypt.

Massive-modern in design;
Functional, graceful each line;
A lofty house to God divine.

In honor of the new synagogue,
Walter L. Field

106

Architect's model of the synagogue complex.
The main element composing the sanctuary
and adjacent halls is on the left; the administrative, school, and service units to the right.

Worship is paramount to the modern
synagogue in America, but the social elements
and the educational element have become of
major importance. So, the synagogue becomes
not merely a house where people assemble to
worship; it becomes a community center, the
single place in the community where the
environment is completely Jewish. The new
Shaarey Zedek buildings clearly show the
tripartite function and the interdependent
relation of each of its parts. The Hall of Prayer
is the dominant element because of its
location and its height. The social halls flank
it and form part of the same structure both
functionally and aesthetically, for these,
though typically halls for festivities, are also
extensions of the prayer hall itself.

Percival Goodman

to those things for which the synagogue stands. "Wherever his destiny has brought him, the Jew's primary purpose has been to build a shrine." Rabbi Groner, looking back over the years, recalls how in those early days people would come to services to sit entranced by the majestic beauty of the sanctuary, whose roof soars over ninety feet over the great ark austerely designed in off-white marble. Dominating the sanctuary, the forty-foot ark is framed by stained glass windows, their colors rising from a deep blue to the curling flames of the burning bush.

The dedication of the synagogue on a Saturday night is not without significance, for the Havdalah service momentarily joins the sacred and the secular in Jewish life: after observing the sanctity of the Sabbath, the congregation is enjoined to reenter the secular realm. And the new synagogue complex was to facilitate bringing the problems of the world into focus through rabbinic sermons, lectures, teaching, and discussion, always within the sanctity of Jewish tradition, thought, and law.

The massive, prow-like form of the sanctuary rises over one of the busiest freeways of the sprawling motor capital, but the entrance to the sanctuary provides an oasis of quiet, synthesizing tradition with the modern world and fulfilling the personal wish of Rabbi Adler. Mrs. Adler remembered, "He felt that the congregation should not just walk off the city street into the sanctuary, that there should be an approach during which you can attune or prepare yourself."

And the magnificent sanctuary was only one factor in the total expression sought by Percival Goodman: "The synagogue was conceived from three viewpoints — as a house of worship, of assembly, and of learning." Shaarey Zedek would seek in the years to come to achieve this unity of expression.

A visual expression of the Jewish community's pride in its heritage and an affirmation of its authentic place in the American landscape, the new building complex is a physical and symbolic landmark in the burgeoning suburbs of Detroit. The move to new quarters served also as a catalyst for enlarging the congregation's family. Four hundred fifty new families, the majority between the ages of twenty-five and forty, joined in the years between 1963 and 1966. The school thus enjoyed a proportionate increase, necessitating almost immediately the addition of six more classrooms. The new housing for the school was promptly supported by curricular changes under the leadership of Eli Grad.

New ways of teaching moral values through the Bible were initiated in the elementary school, and the junior high school was departmentalized to offer more specialized instruction by experts. In 1964-65, girls in the tenth grade for the first time attended a Consecration seminar devoted to the exploration of their future needs as Jewish wives, mothers, and homemakers, and to their role as women in Jewish life. University professors, Hillel directors,

Dear Larry and Elliott:

On this particular morning a handful of men, among them your great, great uncle and your grandfather, gathered together, thirty-five to forty of them, to conduct services at this place for the last time. There was more than one pair of wet eyes as some of the elderly men were called to recite the blessings of the Torah. Larry was the second, and he seemed to symbolize the spirit of the future.

At the customary breakfast after services, Rabbi Adler, in one of his most eloquent and unassuming moments, pointed out the function this small group of men has fulfilled over the years, day in, day out, bad weather, good weather; the daily act of affirmation and loyalty to the faith. Now it was time to leave this building.

In the main sanctuary the Ark stood stripped of its adornments. The Torah scrolls were removed, and the cantor led the small procession of men carrying them up the aisle toward the main entrance. As he did so, he sang melodies from the Hallel. And so we departed for the new sanctuary, choked with emotion. But unlike the passing of an individual where there is a feeling of finality and emptiness, here there was the feeling of rebirth and continuation — the difference between a person and a people.

The occasion was simple and sentimental, a kind of reminder that the strength of our people has not been just in numbers and edifices, but in hard-core devotion and simplicity. We are a people noted for and dedicated to the love of learning; outstanding for our devotion to our communal responsibilities. But we are also a people which has displayed strength in the solitude of shepherds and prophets, in the handful of scholars around a Johanan Ben Zakkai or in the minyans of synagogues large and small.

This was a day when we touched the ages and looked at the face of history.

> *Dad*
> *(Harold Berry)*
>
> *23 Kislev 5723*
> *20 December 1962*

The Congregation Moves

On Thursday morning, December 20, 1962, officers, board members, and synagogue "regulars" attended one of the last services held at the Chicago Boulevard building. Following a brief talk given by Rabbi Adler, the Torah scrolls were removed from the ark, and a procession formed in the main sanctuary; led by Rabbi Adler and Cantor Sonenklar, it left the synagogue through the Chicago Boulevard entrance, with each man holding a Torah scroll in his arms, and boarded the Shaarey Zedek buses for the new synagogue. During the journey, Cantor Sonenklar led the members in singing appropriate psalms and hymns. On reaching the new synagogue, the procession formed once more, and the Torah scrolls were placed in the new sanctuary.

111

.DEA047 SSE085   (53)...

DE WA015 GOVT PD=THE WHITE HOUSE WASHINGTON DC 9 947A EST=

RABBI MORRIS ADLER,   1963 JAN 9 AM 10 0

    CONGREGATION SHAAREY ZEDEK 27375 BELL RD

    SOUTHFIELD MICH=.

I AM PLEASED TO EXTEND TO YOU AND THE MEMBERS OF YOUR CONGREGATION MY WARMEST BEST WISHES AS YOU DEDICATE YOUR NEW SANCTUARY. FOR MORE THAN ONE HUNDRED YEARS, CONGREGATION SHAAREY ZEDEK HAS NOT ONLY TAUGHT THE TRUTHS WHICH ARE PART OF THE SPIRITUAL HERITAGE OF AMERICA, BUT IT HAS ALSO INSTRUCTED MANY GENERATIONS OF ITS MEMBERS IN THE VALUES AND IDEALS UPON WHICH GOOD CITIZENSHIP IN A FREE SOCIETY REST.   1963 JAN 9 AM 10 01

   ¶ YOU AND THE MEMBERS OF CONGREGATION SHAAREY ZEDEK HAVE REASON TO BE BOTH THANKFUL AND PROUD AS YOU DEDICATE YOUR NEW HOUSE OF WORSHIP AND STUDY, AND ON THIS MEMORABLE OCCASION I COMMEND YOU FOR YOUR ACCOMPLISHMENTS AND WISH YOU CONTINUED PROGRESS IN THE YEARS AHEAD=

     JOHN F KENNEDY=

President John F. Kennedy salutes the congregation on the dedication of its new synagogue.

Dedication dinner, January 12, 1963, following a Havdalah service held in the new sanctuary. "The new synagogue, its soaring peak thrust into the wintry sky, will provide dramatic shelter for a people who will commit themselves to be worthy of the magnificent spiritual and cultural home they dedicate" *(The Detroit News).*

Dedication dinner, January 12, 1963; *facing the camera:* Mr. and Mrs. Samuel C. Kovan, Southfield Mayor and Mrs. James Clarkson, President and Mrs. David M. Miro, Mr. and Mrs. Hyman Safran.

High school graduation class, 1962.

and the rabbis of the congregation were among those participating in a seminar for high school seniors that reviewed the basic values of Judaism in relation to the challenges of college life. A science program in cooperation with the Cranbrook Institute of Science was introduced into the Beth Hayeled and pre-kindergarten classes, and a music teacher was added to the staff. Cantor Frankel had an important place in the training of junior chazzanim, Torah readers, and youth choirs among his other duties and instituted a father and son class for Bar Mitzvah candidates to provide both with the opportunity to learn the Bar Mitzvah ceremony. The elementary and junior high students elected their classmates to a Keren Ami council whose function was to plan and implement a program to raise money for various charities and, thus, to learn the very important concept of tsedakah.

A committee was now formed for the reinstitution of an Adult Institute of Jewish Learning. The first classes were well received by the over three hundred registrants who studied Jewish beliefs, the Hebrew language, Jewish music, and American Judaism. Eli Grad added a course on the education of the Jewish child, Cantor Sonenklar a course on the Siddur, and Rabbi Groner a course on Deuteronomy. A highlight of 1965 was a lecture series on American Jewish life that brought in a group of distinguished speakers, many of whom were to become familiar lecturers at the synagogue: Marshall Sklare, Leo Pfeffer, Arthur Hertzberg, Albert Vorspan, and Albert Mayer. New courses on current Jewish issues led by Samuel Krohn and Walter E. Klein, congregants active in the Jewish Community Council, helped make the Adult Education Institute a successful venture in community education.

Jewish education is the synagogue's most sacred task and urgent challenge. For the Jewish parent, it means forging a bond between himself and his children by imparting to them the way of life that binds one generation to the next. For the Jewish child, it means growing up to share in Jewish experiences that link him with his family, both his immediate family and also the extended family of the Jewish people.

Rabbi Irwin Groner

115

Women's choral group, 1963; *first row (left to right):* Cantor Jacob H. Sonenklar, Lois Kahn, Penina Frankel, Selma Feinberg, Evelyn Rudner, Cantor Reuven Frankel; *second row (left to right):* Lillian Olender, Janet Pont, Gail Lutz, Elaine Levin, Lucille Weisberg, Betty Fishman, Leypsa Groner; *third row (left to right):* Geri Levit, Marilyn Rollinger, Ruth Podolsky, Adeline Lachman, Leah Baum, Jean Goren, Marge Ruby.

The Fine Arts Commission can stimulate a greater awareness of the development of Jewish art and plan carefully a program for the aesthetic enrichment of our congregational life. The synagogue as the center of Jewish religious life should be the repository of Jewish art and subsequently must take the lead in translating holiness to beauty.

Max M. Shaye, chairman

The Sisterhood, some seventy years young, continued as an indispensible affiliate of the congregational family, building the sukkah each year, preparing the Bar Mitzvah kiddush, serving in the gift shop, and raising funds for the many synagogue needs. In 1963-64, it initiated morning classes in written and spoken Hebrew.

The "Book of the Brunch Club" series featured book reviews given by Goldie Adler. By popular demand she gave a book review one evening in 1963 to which both men and women were invited, and over twelve hundred people filled the social hall. In the same year, Mrs. Adler was honored at a tea celebrating her twenty-five years of service to the Sisterhood and to the congregation.

The great influx of young families into the synagogue had the greatest impact on the Young Married League, which took on new obligations of service. Hootenannys, square dances and skating parties not only served to bring the new young families into the synagogue family, but also prepared them for the important roles they would assume as leaders in the coming decades.

A committee on social issues formed, following the commandment to Micah. Meetings were held with public school educators, inquiry was made into current civil rights legislation, open housing was studied and strongly supported, and the principle of equal opportunity adopted and practiced. Social issues served to translate the moral duties of the synagogue into the idiom of today's society.

In 1964-65, under the chairmanship of Max M. Shaye, the Fine Arts Commission was formed to stimulate an awareness of Jewish art and to plan a program of aesthetic enrichment. The group had a three-fold purpose: to acquire Jewish art for the synagogue, to plan programs of art appreciation, and to enrich the cultural life of the community. A fine arts fund was established, and the first annual Shaarey Zedek art show was hung.

Presentation of *Procession,* by Arthur Schneider, to the congregation by Mr. and Mrs. Abraham Borman in 1965.

The Youth Committee and the four children's congregations (Children: ages 4-7; Intermediate: ages 8-11; Tikvah: ages 12-13; Junior: ages 14-17) expanded their activities, and a scouting program for boys and girls was reestablished. Another addition to the congregation's growing number of programs was a Young Adult Group for single members between the ages of twenty-one and thirty-five; various camping programs at the synagogue and at Camp Ramah flourished.

Symbolic of the vitality of the congregation's renewed energy was the award given to the Men's Club in 1965 by the National Federation of Jewish Men's Clubs for the best all-around programming. The Men's Club had maintained its everyday obligations to the synagogue, serving as ushers, participating in the morning minyans, sponsoring youth activities, and raising funds. But its members were also deeply concerned in exploring the social, moral, and political issues of the day. Such authorities as Rabbi Eugene Lipman and Warren Moscow were brought to the synagogue. Nor did the members of the Men's Club forget the pleasures of their Jewish and Yiddish heritage; Harry Golden was brought to the synagogue to quicken any failing memory. Significant for the future of the synagogue's ceremony was the decision by the Men's Club to join with their wives in a panel discussion on the question of modifying the ritual. This issue, central to the Conservative

November 15, 1961. Congregation Shaarey
Zedek receives the Solomon Schecter Award
in the areas of elementary and high school
education at the United Synagogue of America
convention held at Kiamesha Lake, New York.
Left to right: Dr. and Mrs. Samuel Krohn,
Howard S. Danzig, Abe Birenbaum, president
of Shaarey Zedek Abraham Satovsky, Dr.
Louis Finkelstein, Rabbi and Mrs. Morris
Adler, Daniel C. Cullen, Mrs. Abraham
Satovsky, Mrs. Daniel C. Cullen.

In 1974, President and Mrs. Robert A.
Steinberg accept the Solomon Schecter Award
for the congregational Learning Resource
Center from Henry N. Rapaport, honorary
president of the United Synagogue of America,
and Arthur J. Levine, president of the United
Synagogue of America.

Repeat performance: a Solomon Schecter Award for the Beth Hayeled and library programs in 1979. *Left to right:* Ruth Rice; Russell Gilson; Jacqueline Milgrom; Joseph Deutch; Elsie Deutch; Rosaline Gilson, director of the Beth Hayeled; Myron L. Milgrom; Nancy Baron; Dennis Rice; Rabbi Irwin Groner; Leonard E. Baron.

movement, was decided in favor of retaining, for the time being, the ceremonial program as it had been in the Chicago Boulevard building.

On January 4, 1964, Rabbi Adler received from President David M. Miro the thanks of his congregants for twenty-five years of service. In his honor, the east social hall was designated the Morris Adler Hall, "in our everlasting appreciation for devotion and service to Congregation Shaarey Zedek." Among those who paid tribute to the rabbi were Governor George Romney, Judge Wade McCree, Dr. Henry Hitt Crane, Walter Reuther, and Dr. Max Arzt of The Jewish Theological Seminary of America. Behind all of the activity of the congregation stood Rabbi Adler. He was the driving force for the construction of the new synagogue; his vision, determination, and ceaseless work inspired the lay leaders to raise a seemingly impossible amount of money and to work with the architects and various commissions almost on a full-time basis.

Rabbi Adler's vision was clear: the great structure, while necessary for a growing congregation, was not an end in itself; its true purpose lay not in bricks and mortar but in the conduct and attitudes of the families it housed. Rabbi Adler lived in the present world, a disturbing world of profound turbulence in the early sixties, but he also lived in the world of his Fathers, reminding the congregants that to do justly today one must understand and apply the wisdom and tradition of the ages.

Rabbi Adler died on March 11, 1966, after being critically wounded during the Bar Mitzvah services of February 12. Only three weeks before, he had composed a prescient poem. Goldie Adler remembers how deeply moved he had been by the tragic deaths of several young members of a Temple Beth El family. After a visit to the bereaved, Rabbi Adler had secluded himself in his

"Tribute to a Teacher." On January 4, 1964, Rabbi Adler is honored for his twenty-five years of service. National figures gathered in tribute in recognition of his participation not only in the synagogue, but in such community services as the Citizens Committee for Equal Opportunity, the Detroit Round Table of Christians and Jews, the Community Health Association, and the Governor's Committee for Higher Education as well.

Louis Berry and David M. Miro of Shaarey Zedek join Walter Reuther and Governor George Romney to pose with the rabbi. Also present during the Havdalah ceremony were Judge Wade McCree, Dr. Henry Hitt Crane, and Dr. Max Arzt of The Jewish Theological Seminary of America.

To perpetuate evidence of our everlasting appreciation for your devotion and service to Congregation Shaarey Zedek, from this time on the auditorium area adjacent to our main sanctuary shall be known as the Morris Adler Hall.

David M. Miro, president

The "klay-kodesh" of the synagogue, January 4, 1964: Rabbi Irwin Groner, Cantor Reuven Frankel, Rabbi Morris Adler, and Cantor Jacob H. Sonenklar at the "Tribute to a Teacher" which honored Rabbi Adler's twenty-fifth anniversary at Shaarey Zedek.

study. In the early hours of the morning he read his poem to his wife.

> Shall I cry out in anger, O God,
> Because thy gifts are mine
>   but for a while. . . .
> What Thou givest O Lord
> Thou takest not away
> And bounties once granted
> Shed their radiance evermore.
> Within me youth, love and vision
> Now woven deep into the texture
> Live and will be mine; till Thou
> callest me hence
> To another realm,
>   where these moments of eternity
> Shall be joined together
> In unbroken sequence
> To form eternal life.

First appearing in the *Recorder*, the poem was reprinted in *The Jewish News* to give strength to a grieving community.

Two weeks before the shocking murder, Rabbi Adler had written about alienated youth, affirming his belief that while alienation was a function of adolescence, there was more to the turmoil and unsettledness than that.

> Alienation or maladjustment need not be the exclusive consequence of the psychic weaknesses of the subject; they may be understandable reactions to the inadequacy of the object. In other words, the failure of society may be a root cause no less or perhaps more than the instability of the juvenile rebels.

The event received nation-wide attention; here only the simple fact need be reported. A disturbed young congregant who revered the rabbi had come up onto the bima that Saturday of February 12, shot the rabbi, and then taken his own life.

The rabbi had said when speaking of the youth of the sixties, "We are inducing them into a life in which insecurity and apprehension are dominant, so that the future holds out for them no promising possibilities of peace, safety, and security." Goldie Adler understood her husband's words. Through those weeks of constant vigil by his bedside, and still today, her compassion and concern for the parents of the troubled youth have overriden her sense of personal loss. Goldie Adler set the example for the congregation, to live and to act with courage, compassion, and restraint.

Rabbi Adler's preeminent position in the community and nationally and the unspeakable tragedy of his death combined to produce a funeral whose proportions were exceeded only by the depth of mourning. The sanctuary was filled to capacity; mourners crowded the building and stood outside. Among the mourners sat many not of the congregation who had been close friends, colleagues in the never-ending struggle for social justice, long-time

In Israel, when a distinguished man has been called from this life, some thirty days later an assembly is held, or a meeting is arranged, even at the grave, and friends and associates and acquaintances are invited to come to commune with his spirit, to stand apart from life and dedicate themselves for a moment, to live in the presence of the great man's memory. The community of which we are a part comprises many more than those who are visible. A community has continuity and time, and it includes all those who have preceded us and have left their imprint upon our collective life.

Americans will this day seek to commune with the presence of perhaps the greatest American we have ever produced. Lincoln was not only a man great in powers of the mind, a man who was able to put words together like a prayer, as he did at Gettysburg and in his second inaugural address; he was also a man of heart. There is no other person in our history who impresses one as being a man of such compassion, a man of such intense feeling as this man of sorrow, whose sorrow was the sorrow of all. "I have not only suffered for the South," he once said, "I have suffered with the South."

He was a man who had the greatness of faith, but he was probably the only president who did not belong to a church. And yet he stimulates a sense of intense faith. He was probably the most religious, though the least traditional, of all the men we have called to our highest office, and in his religion, as in his life, there was directness and simplicity. The symbols and rituals and doctrines that so often obscure the vital power and basic message of religion were not for him.

Abraham Lincoln was a man of faith. He did not think that God approved of everything he did, and he did not think that he knew all about God, or that God belonged exclusively to him. He once said, "In great contests, each party claims to act in accordance with the will of God. Both may be, and one must be, wrong. God cannot be for and against the same thing at the same time. In the present Civil War it is quite possible that God's purpose is something different from the purposes of either party."

From the last sermon of Rabbi Morris Adler; February 12, 1966

Rabbi Morris Adler, 1906-1966.

associates in the clergy and civic groups: Governor and Mrs. George Romney; Lieutenant Governor William Milliken; former Governor G. Mennen Williams; Senator Philip Hart; Mayor Jerome Cavanaugh; Judges Theodore Levin, George Edwards, and Horace Gilmore; Walter Reuther and his family; and the Reverends G. Merrill Lenox, Clement Kern, and George Higgins. Dr. Louis Finkelstein, chancellor of The Jewish Theological Seminary of America, asked in his eulogy, "What better way is there to die than at the moment when one has been expressing his love for God and his love for his fellow man?" Rabbi Groner, presiding over the service, answered the unspoken question that hovered as a shadow above the assembly: "In his memory we will find the strength to go forward into the uncertainties of the future."

The synagogue's Clover Hill Park Cemetery is the setting for the memorial monument designed by Sol King of the Albert Kahn and Associates architectural company, who has briefly described it.

> The monument is a simple, white marble block, low in height in order to direct the visitor's eye downward. The block is capped by an open book symbolizing learning (Torah). The curved form of the book's pages, together with the sloping sides of the block, create a single entity suggesting the Tablets. The inscription is placed near the bottom of the block in order to force the visitor to gaze further downward. And yet the surrounding elements emphasize the open sky, and stimulate one also to turn to heaven. The visitor is always set back into shadow as he views the open and sunlit memorial. This is not only appropriate to physical comfort, but is an essential part of the meaning of the design.

The inscription is poignant in its brevity.

> A flame of Spirit he was
> Before its Time consumed
> His light is with us yet
> When shall we see his like again?
> Rabbi Morris Adler, 1906-1966

The trauma of this great tragedy was felt not only by the congregation and the greater Detroit community, but also by the nation and world at large. Rabbi Adler had been a leader in virtually all areas of Jewish and community life. How did the congregation come to terms with their rabbi's shocking and inexplicable death? Rabbi Groner explains that Rabbi Adler left a living legacy, that in memory to him the synagogue has grown from strength to strength, exhibiting the best that was within all. And the congregation also recognizes the critical role played by Rabbi Groner in assuming the position of rabbi of the synagogue. Perhaps no task in a religious community is more difficult than successfully to assume the position of a beloved spiritual leader suddenly taken from the congregation.

Irwin Groner, elected rabbi of the synagogue
April 17, 1967.

Rabbi Groner had received his degrees from the University of Chicago and the Hebrew Theological College of Chicago, where he was ordained, and had served as rabbi of the Agudath Achim congregation in Little Rock, Arkansas, before coming to Shaarey Zedek as assistant rabbi in 1959. Subsequently he has gone on to receive an honorary doctorate from The Jewish Theological Seminary of America and to serve as secretary of the Rabbinical Assembly of America, co-chairman of the National Youth Commission of the United Synagogue, vice-president of the Jewish Community Council of Detroit, and as a member of the editorial committee for *The New Mahzor* (High Holy Day Prayer Book) published in 1977. He and his wife Leypsa have three children, Deborah, David, and Joel. A man of dignity, spirituality, and intellectual depth, Rabbi Groner has used his leadership as a subtle catalyst, comforting a mourning congregation and spurring it on to new ventures within the context of the Conservative movement.

Rabbi Adler's chair on the bima remained empty, his study door closed, as the congregation mourned his death for one year. Rabbi Groner, who served as acting rabbi during this year, was elected rabbi of the congregation at the 106th annual meeting of the congregation on April 17, 1967. With strength, compassion, and insight that belied his thirty-five years, he assumed the spiritual leadership with the talmudic words that those who are pained by the distress of the community will be rewarded by sharing in the comfort and fulfillment of that community.

And so the congregation drew ever closer together in 1967, sharing its grief, but at the same time reaffirming the biblical challenge to choose life. The Rabbi Morris Adler Memorial Foundation was established to support those religious, charitable, and educational projects that were dear to his heart. A testament to the importance placed on education was the successful formation of a Hebrew Teachers' Association whose contract formalized many of the provisions of the personnel code and practices already in existence at Shaarey Zedek. Salary and benefits were to be the highest in the country. Joshua Weinstein became educational director that year, replacing Eli Grad, who became head of Hebrew College in Boston.

The several committees of the congregation had resumed their activities, guided by the administrative skill of Howard S. Danzig, executive director, who came to Shaarey Zedek in 1961. Dialogues on human relations in a modern society, a seminar on the moral and ethical challenges in medical practice, an exhibition of great modern Jewish artists, a premier performance of a sacred oratorio directed by Dan Frohman, who had long served the congregation as music director, and a two-day conference on the woman's world crowded the calendar.

The year of mourning ended, and the families and staff of Shaarey Zedek moved on with increased energy, drawing upon the

Rabbi and Mrs. Irwin Groner.
Leypsa Groner, who shares the joys and sorrows of the congregational family with her husband, Rabbi Groner, is an accomplished pianist; Mrs. Groner accompanies the Sisterhood choir and assists the Consecration class.

At the dinner marking the tenth anniversary of the new synagogue, some five hundred members watched a Havdalah ceremony conducted by the Junior Congregation. In the Ceremony of Remembrance, Rabbi Irwin Groner narrated the outstanding events of the ten years while ten children, each ten years old, lit a candle on the birthday cake: Wendy Joyrich, Steven Schwartz, Nathan Forbes, Marc Bortnick, Daniel Stulberg, Judith Brown, Steven Moss, Douglas Levine, David Elkus, Miriam Steinberg. Mr. Morris Fishman lit the eleventh candle and recited with the members the traditional benediction of thanksgiving.

moral legacy of the rabbi whose portrait, painted by Detroiter Ben Glicker, now hung in the Board Room.

But the 1960s and 1970s were difficult years in which to perpetuate a sense of stability in the rough seas of massive social change. Rabbi Groner articulated the belief of his congregation that love of God, love of Torah, and love for one another transcend all even in crisis, confusion, and the turmoil of change. He was given life tenure as rabbi of Shaarey Zedek in 1978, a fitting spiritual heir to Rabbis Hershman and Adler. His ability to resist the temptation of change for its own sake has provided the congregation with a sound sense of continuity.

This feeling of continuity has given form and meaning to the many anniversary celebrations of the synagogue. The tenth year in the new building complex was a time for rejoicing and remembrance. Some five hundred members joined in the formal celebration on January 20, 1973. Appropriately, ten children, each ten years old, lit the candles on the birthday cake, followed by Morris Fishman, a respected elder of the congregation, who lit the eleventh candle for the future. Three years later, the 115th anniversary of the synagogue was ushered in for a year-long festivity. The theme, *dor l'dor,* from one generation to another, found expression in an oral history project. Members of the Junior Congregation and college students interviewed senior members of the congregation who reminisced about Shaarey Zedek in the early years of this century and recounted tales of their lives in Europe before they came to America. The project offered a singular opportunity for communication between the generations as well as valuable historical documentation. The 115th anniversary dinner on December 12,

Rabbi Irwin Groner, Walter L. Field, and Mandell L. Berman at the 115th anniversary celebration, December 12, 1976.

This has been a decade of discontinuities, of violent breaks in the flow of history. They came in almost every vital area of society — in the pattern of the family, in the idea of God, in the life of the cities and the suburbs, in the deterioration of our environment, in the attitudes toward law and authority, in the generational struggle and the inner world of the young.

This has been a decade of alienation, a time of ideological confusion, with a pervading crisis of belief and with new cults of the irrational and the bizarre.

This has been a decade when our congregation has prayed together, wept together, rejoiced together, failed together, and achieved together. The essence of our synagogue resides in the covenant that love of God, love of Torah, and love for one another transcends all, even in crisis, in confusion, and in the turmoil of change.

> *Rabbi Irwin Groner,*
> *on the occasion of the*
> *tenth anniversary in the*
> *Southfield synagogue buildings, 1973*

Congregation
Shaarey Zedek

115th
Anniversary
Celebration
1861 - 1976

December 12, 1976
21 Kislev 5737.

Preparing for Bar Mitzvah with Cantor
Sidney Rube.

Irwin Weisberg demonstrates the binding
of tefellin.

1976, witnessed candle-lighting by six fifth-generation families,
the oldest and the youngest in each family lighting a candle
together. *Dor l'dor* — from one generation to another.

The synagogue set itself three major goals in the last two decades: to deal with social change while maintaining the religious
link with the past, to remain fiscally sound in a time of skyrocket-
ing inflation, and to provide a sense of belonging, a feeling of relevance and purpose. As the seventies began, each of the presidents
contributed his unique skills toward achieving these goals: Samuel
Krohn his deep sense of Jewish service, Max. L. Lichter his ability
to develop leadership teams, and Robert A. Steinberg his personal
warmth and contagious enthusiasm. But above all the synagogue is
a house of worship. Conservative Judaism has never been static. It

Bat Mitzvah.

has grown at a serene and steady pace. The Ritual Committee, later called the Religious Services Committee, was created in 1968 to explore and recommend ways in which the services might be expanded or altered to enable a maximum of congregational participation without altering the basic structure of Conservative Jewish ritual. Bar Mitzvah parents now ascend the bima with their child. Women have been brought into the choir, and late Friday evening services have been reinstituted with the chorale of mixed voices. The reading of the Torah portion has been modified in order to accommodate commentary and interpretation. In 1974 the Sephardic pronunciation, that of modern Israel, replaced the Ashkenazic in the prayer services.

Further changes have been made to bring the congregation out of the role of spectator into that of participant. Aliyot are given to the father of the consecrant who offers the prayer for our country at

Consecration class, 1968.

Consecration class, 1970.

Sabbath services. Newlyweds and new parents are recognized from the pulpit, and more members are invited to participate in pulpit functions.

The role of women in the synagogue has become a major focus in the Conservative movement. Hence, several times during the decade the very complex issue of Bat Mitzvah had been broached and then dropped. Rabbi Groner and the Religious Services Committee understood the desire of girls to express themselves, to participate in Sabbath services. And so the Bat Torah program was instituted in 1977-78, and honors students in the Consecration class gave sermonettes on the Sabbath. Then, in 1980, the Bat Mitzvah was initiated at the Friday night services of May 16; more than thirty girls have marked the event and accepted the obligation for continued study through Consecration. Girls are given the opportunity to observe their Bat Mitzvah, but they are not compelled to do so. Those who do not wish to deviate from traditional roles are not to be made uncomfortable in their choice.

Women have assumed increased responsibility, sitting on the

"Operation Alef-Bet," a Hebrew literacy program which began in the fall of 1980 under the auspices of the Sisterhood and the Men's Club. The course, in which 190 students were taught by 15 volunteers, was so successful that the Cultural Commission offered an additional course, Alef-Bet Step II (Pathways through the Siddur), which featured a videotape of selected prayers sung by a volunteer choir, with commentary by Cantor Najman and Rabbi Groner.

The music division of the Cultural Commission meets at the Hermelin home in 1977.

Board and participating in services throughout the year. Change comes gradually after thoughtful deliberation and within the context of tradition.

Soon after Rabbi Groner's election, Walter L. Field, a forty-year member of the congregation, proposed developing a comprehensive program for enlarging and expanding the values of Jewish learning and culture by the creation of a Cultural Commission. The organizing committee met in the rabbi's study on July 10, 1967, and evolved a well-planned program which was soon to become the prototype for synagogue programming for both the

131

"Havdalah," a new work by the well-known composer Morton Gold presented at Shaarey Zedek in 1980 and sponsored by Peter and Clara Weisberg. The concert featured Cantor Chaim Najman as the soloist and Rabbi Irwin Groner as the narrator; the choral portions were sung by the Shaarey Zedek Adult and Youth Choirs.

November 14, 1971: Walter L. Field, chairman of the Cultural Commission, and Rabbi Irwin Groner accept the Solomon Schecter Award for outstanding adult education programming in behalf of Congregation Shaarey Zedek from Dr. Jacob Stein, president of the United Synagogue of America.

On a rabbinic mission to Israel in February, 1969, Rabbi Groner meets Russian-Jewish refugees at the Lod Airport.

community and the country, one which placed the new commission at the center of adult programming. Seated on its executive committee were the presidents of the Sisterhood, the Men's Club, and the Young Married League, and the chairmen and co-chairmen of the new divisions (with the rabbis and cantors as ex-officio members). Four divisions were formed, replacing three existing committees and adding a fourth on education (Home Discussion Division). The commission stressed programs, open to the public and free of charge, that involved as many members as possible.

Among the best-known programs sponsored by members are the Walter and Lea Field history lectures, the Davidson family Great Weekend series, the Berry family Spring Lectures, the Irwin T. Holtzman family Israeli speakers, the Adolph M. Lichter Memorial Lectures, the Peter and Clara Weisberg musical events, and the Morris Adler Memorial Foundation Lectures. A procession of fine Jewish scholars, artists, and leaders ascended the podium — among them Salo Baron, Maurice Samuel, Mordecai Kaplan, Abraham

133

Sisterhood choral group, 1980-81.

Heschel, Robert Gordis, Isaac Bashevis Singer, Elie Wiesel, Gerson D. Cohen, Chaim Potok, Simon Wiesenthal, David Sidorsky, Marshall Sklare, Emil Fackenheim — a veritable who's who of Jewry. One particularly memorable event was a concert given by a twenty-five-year-old Russian émigré who had been a pupil of David Oistrakh. Sponsored by Cantor Jacob Barkin, who brought him to the attention of the local and national musical world, Alexander Treger made his debut on January 16, 1974, at a concert in the synagogue sanctuary.

The decade of the 1970s witnessed a deepening of concern with Soviet Jewry, for their rescue and relief. Certainly prayers had been offered for Soviet Jewry, but the stirring words of Elie Wiesel at the spring lecture series in 1970 mobilized the congregation to action. The Men's Club sponsored a trip to Washington enabling members of the Junior Congregation to participate in the Youth Mobilization for Soviet Jewry. The next several months witnessed vigorous protest, prayer, and physical support at almost every level of the synagogue. Several Russian Jewish families were "adopted" and provided with the support necessary to bring them to this country. Two Bar Mitzvahs that took place in 1980 have a particular poignancy. Mikhail Kosharovsky, the son of one of the Soviet Union's leading Hebrew teachers, who with his family had been trying to emigrate since 1971, had his Bar Mitzvah by proxy at Shaarey Zedek. A month later, four generations of Russian Jews recently arrived from Kishinev attended the Bar Mitzvah of Mikhail Stern. His ninety-year-old great-grandmother, who recited all the prayers from memory, exclaimed that she had never dreamed she might again attend a synagogue without fear.

Israel, of course, remains of primary importance. The Irwin T. Holtzman family events brought the writers Yehuda Amichai,

134

Israel Bonds Dinner (Trade Union dinner), June 21, 1962, Cobo Hall; *left to right:* Max M. Fisher, Eleanor Roosevelt, Rabbi Morris Adler.

The 1969 Israel Bond Dinner honored past presidents of the congregation. *Seated (left to right):* Abraham Satovsky, Hyman Safran, Leonard Sidlow, Charles Rubiner, Harry Cohen; *standing (left to right):* Irwin Green, dinner chairman; Rabbi Irwin Groner; Samuel C. Kovan; David M. Miro; Louis Berry.

"Let Your House Be a Meeting Place for Sages"

In Jewish tradition, one studies and learns so that one may do justly. The scholars and leaders brought to Shaarey Zedek by the Cultural Commission to share their wisdom and understanding of the current condition of the Jew have been greeted by standing room-only crowds, from college students to senior citizens, drawn not only from the congregation but from the Jewish community at large as well.

Cecil Roth

William F. Albright

Mordechai Kaplan

Abraham Kaplan

Arthur Lelyveld

Harry Orlinsky

Maurice Samuel

Mark Van Doren

Gerson D. Cohen

Salo Baron

Abraham Heschel

Elie Wiesel

Chaim Potok

Arthur Hertzberg

Abraham Sachar

Isaac Bashevis Singer

Leon Jick

Allen Pollock

137

Throughout its one hundred twenty years the congregation has maintained a vital interest in the community and the world beyond. David W. Simons, for example, served on the city of Detroit's council as well as serving as president of Shaarey Zedek. National and international civic leaders have been invited to the synagogue to lecture and participate in seminars; the congregation has searched out in the United States and abroad those who can inform and deepen the members' understanding of life in the twentieth century.

Abba Eban came to Shaarey Zedek to speak at a bond drive, Senator Daniel Patrick Moynihan to present the Adolph Lichter Memorial Lecture. During a 1979 convocation in Florida, Rabbi Groner had the opportunity to talk with Senator Howard Baker and Dr. Gerson D. Cohen, chancellor of The Jewish Theological Seminary of America. President Carter met with the rabbi and other Jewish leaders in Washington. Study tours and visits to Israel form an important part of the congregants' Jewish education. In 1969 Rabbi Groner joined his colleagues Rabbi Richard C. Hertz of Temple Beth El and Rabbi James I. Gordon of Young Israel on the east bank of the Suez Canal, and Menachim Begin and his grandchild greeted Rabbi and Mrs. Groner in Jerusalem during Purim of 1974, when a synagogue group toured Israel.

139

The Shaarey Zedek Shomrim. *First row (left to right):* Harvey L. Weisberg; Peter Weisberg; Meyer Fishman; Louis Berry; Cantor Jacob Barkin; Harold Berry, president of Shaarey Zedek; Rabbi Irwin Groner; Samuel Hamburger; Nathan Fishman; Joseph H. Jackier; Henry Dorfman. *Second row (left to right):* Milford Nemer, Jay M. Kogan, Thomas Borman, Hyman Safran, Joseph B. Slatkin, Max M. Shaye, William B. Davidson, Dennis Rice, Walter L. Field, Edward Fleischman, Malcolm E. Lowenstein, Irwin Green, Louis Hamburger. Absent: Max M. Fisher, Joseph Frenkel, A. Alfred Taubman.

Amos Oz, and A. B. Yehoshua to speak. The works of Israeli artists such as Yaacov Agam and Shalom of Safed were exhibited through the efforts of the music and art division. The annual Israel bonds dinners are a testament to the generosity of the membership.

The spirit of tolerance and social consciousness that marks the congregation is continually visible in such modest, but important, events as inviting Christian churches to visit the Sabbath services, or in the exchange-visit program between the Beth Hayeled and youngsters in a Protestant church, or in the Sisterhood's annual "brotherhood" teas. But one special occasion stands out. St. Ives Church wished to hold a dinner dance as a fund-raising activity but found its own facility too small. So Shaarey Zedek opened its social hall to the more than four hundred Protestants, Catholics, and Jews who came to this event. "The thought of a group of Catholics with the full knowledge and consent of the parish priest using the social hall of a Jewish synagogue was not just unthinkable," reported a local newspaper. "It was close to heretical not too many years ago."

Social change, almost too rapid for the mind to absorb, was the ongoing reality of the past two decades. The youth rebellion became the subject of symposia, lectures, and an Outreach program to students at Michigan universities who were members of the Shaarey Zedek family. The Men's Club sponsored a series of Wednesday luncheons to discuss coping with our changing morality, while the Sisterhood investigated the changing role of women under the pressure of women's liberation movements and the ERA campaign.

Among the many landmark years in the recent history of Shaarey Zedek, that of 1976 stands out as one of unique importance, both because it marked the 115th anniversary of the congregation and because this was the year in which the mortgage on the new building came due; in this year the mortgage was paid in full. Sparked by the initial concept of Walter L. Field, Rabbi Groner formed a fellowship of twenty-four men, the Shaarey Zedek Shomrim, who generously paid the remaining mortgage.

In the following year another group of sixty-three members, the

Harold Berry presents Rabbi Groner with an Israeli gold commemorative coin on the successful completion of the Shomrim program. William M. Davidson, Leonard E. Baron, Harvey L. Weisberg, and David B. Hermelin look on.

The first Shaarey Zedek Endowment Board (Chaverim trustees). *First row (left to right):* Rabbi Irwin Groner, David B. Hermelin, Harold Berry, Walter L. Field, Peter A. Martin, William M. Davidson; *second row (left to right):* Harvey L. Weisberg, Myron L. Milgrom, Irving Laker, Robert A. Steinberg.

Chaverim, formed to pay off a short-term bank debt and to establish an endowment fund. The project was successfully completed under the vigorous leadership of Shaarey Zedek president William B. Davidson, who became the first chairman of the newly established Endowment Board in 1981. A third group, the Menadvim or donors, composed a fellowship of members who would remember the congregation with a legacy or bequest of twenty-five thousand dollars or more. The income from this endowment was to be used for special programs and new projects outside the operational budget of the synagogue. Finally, the long-felt need for a reserve with sufficient resources to assure the congregation's welfare in years to come was beginning to be met.

These were anxious decades, crowded with problems and their resolutions, with the need to change and the need to preserve tradition. However, the most challenging problem for the synagogue came, not from the sudden crises which bind members together for the moment, nor from the setting of grand goals which demand unity of action, but in less spectacular dress. The ability to transform a community of several thousand persons into intimate

Jewish education through the ages has been characterized by several qualities. First, education is linked with life. Second, Jewish tradition emphasizes reverence for learning. Third, Jewish education is a life-long process. These historic values have found renewed expression and emphasis in the P.T.O. of Congregation Shaarey Zedek Religious Schools. The P.T.O. has sought to reinforce and reemphasize the partnership of parent and teacher in the religious education of the Jewish child. Parents can help shape the attitudes of reverence for Jewish education and respect for the teacher so indispensable for positive achievement. The P.T.O., in pursuance of the goal embodied in the motto "And thou shall teach them diligently unto thy children," has stressed the importance of the home in reinforcing the values taught in the religious school.

Rabbi Irwin Groner

groupings, each with a sense of purpose, is the central challenge for any large synagogue in a society which offers a multitude of avenues for self-expression. In an era when doing one's own thing seemed to take precedence, the congregation made a conscious effort to provide outlets for expression for each member, young and old. Clergy and lay officers were determined that there be a place for everyone at Shaarey Zedek.

Thus, a Couples Club emerged, and the Home Studies Division expanded to include small discussion groups in music and art. A new Parent-Teacher Organization was formed in 1980, providing young parents with the opportunity to play a part in the shaping of their children's religious education. One of the most recent and most creative groupings within the synagogue, both locally and nationally, is the Chavurah movement. Begun in 1976 by Rabbi Howard V. Lifshitz, in the following year the Chavurah movement had grown to thirteen groups functioning within the synagogue, with three more in formation. The Chavurah provide a means by which families can share in Jewish experience, joining together for Sabbath dinners, holiday celebrations, and study and worship, thus providing the nuclear family with a sense of extended familial participation in Jewish life.

The sensitivity of the congregation to those cultural values which are uniquely possessed by man is typified by the manner in which the members chose to honor Cantor Jacob H. Sonenklar, who had become emeritus in 1969. On his eightieth birthday, in 1974, the Cantor Jacob H. Sonenklar Fund was established to assist in developing a music section in the synagogue library. Trained in

Rabbi: *from the Hebrew, Master, a Teacher.*

High school graduation class, 1978.

The mantle of responsibility borne by a rabbi is made lighter by the privilege of representing the congregation in honoring those who have served the synagogue, the community, and greater Judaism.

Myron L. Milgrom and I. Murray Jacobs received distinguished service awards from The Jewish Theological Seminary of America in 1978 and 1979.

Louis Berry, Rabbi Irwin Groner, and Morris Karbal at the 12th annual Academic Convocation of The Jewish Theological Seminary of America held in Miami Beach on February 28, 1971. Mr. Karbal, secretary of the congregation, received the Community Service Award.

Cantor Chaim Najman celebrates a
Bar Mitzvah.

Austria and under the famous Chazzan Weinman of Tarnow, Cantor Sonenklar studied on a scholarship at the Conservatory of
Music in Vienna before undertaking his first cantorial position in
Romania; in Chicago he served at Congregations Dorshe Tov and
Amshe Emet. From his appointment in 1932 until his retirement
in 1969, he literally was the "voice" of the congregation. He was
succeeded by Cantor Jacob Barkin who, after studies at the Toronto
Conservatory and Eastman School of Music, established himself as
a concert singer. Cantor Barkin, one of the guiding spirits of the
congregation's cultural commissions, officiated for the last time
before retirement at the Sabbath services of December 23, 1978.
Cantor Chaim Najman currently holds this post and also serves as
music director of Shaarey Zedek. Among his many contributions
to the musical life of the congregation are the revitalized Sisterhood Chorale, the Men's Club Choir, the newly formed Youth
Choir, the congregational Choir for Friday evening services, and a
new music program in the Shaarey Zedek school.

145

Rabbi Groner and Beth Hayeled students.

Child: "Rabbi, who made the night and who made the day?"
Rabbi: "God did this."
Child: "Who made the sun; who made the moon; who made the stars?"
Rabbi: "It was God who made all these."
Children: "We know Him. He goes to our school."

Albert E. Karbal and young students at the Learning Resource Center, a unique educational milieu which offers library and audiovisual materials and educational aids.

146

Rabbi Gerald A. Teller engages the Junior Congregation in discussion at their annual Kibbutz at Camp Tamarack.

The heritage of the synagogue must be preserved and passed on to the future generation. Hence, the congregation's children are a primary concern, from the Beth Hayeled program through the Outreach to students on college campuses. Each is urged to become an integral part of his or her religion and its observance. Nothing in the services and religious activities of the synagogue is off-limits to the young, for they insure the congregation a future generation of committed and active Jews. The educational director of the synagogue bears responsibility for this vital aspect of Shaarey Zedek's community. Joshua Weinstein ably served in this capacity and was succeeded by Rabbi Gerald A. Teller in 1970. In response to Rabbi Teller's call for innovative programs, the Sisterhood provided the means to establish the Learning Resource Center, directed by Albert E. Karbal. This media center provides the most advanced forms of audio-visual techniques for the interpretation and expression of Jewish education and values.

Running the Purim carnival, decorating the sukkah, conducting the annual Youth Sabbath, belonging to the United Synagogue Youth with participation in regional meetings and intermural sporting events, and raising funds for various projects are visible signs of a vital youth program. A new JIFY (Jewish Institute for Youth) program for youngsters of high school age, established by

147

"Le-had-lik ner shel Shabbat.
Bo-ray P'ri Ha-Gafen."

Dr. Simon Schwartz, president of the United Synagogue of America, presents a citation to Congregation Shaarey Zedek in recognition of its 120th anniversary on November 18, 1981; *left to right:* Dr. Simon Schwartz, Rabbi Irwin Groner, Harvey L. Weisberg, Thomas Jablonski.

Rabbi Alan B. Lucas, has proved successful, offering lectures given by guest speakers on topics ranging from "Judaism and Islam" to "Interdating and Intermarriage." Leonard E. Baron, president of the congregation from 1979-81, served at a time when there was no executive director and no educational director, placing an unusual administrative burden on his shoulders. During his term of office a branch school was established at the Greenfield Elementary School in West Bloomfield Township. As an increasing number of members moved farther west into this area, the problem of transporting youngsters to the synagogue during the mid-week late afternoon and early evening hours had become increasingly acute, recommending the creation of branch classrooms.

No one moment in the history of a synagogue provides a clear image of the congregation, beause a synagogue is a living entity, always changing and growing, as President Harvey L. Weisberg noted in his message to the congregation at the beginning of its one hundred and twentieth year. While it is true that the present generation may not hold the synagogue as central to its life as did the founding families of Shaarey Zedek, the intense activity and interest expressed by the modern congregation in Jewish ideals and service are little diminished. It is this spirit, this vitality, that Robert A. Steinberg, past president of the synagogue, articulated in recounting the day when a group of Catholic parishioners were visiting the new buildings. Their priest remarked on the splendid leadership of the synagogue. Their guide responded that a building has no meaning except that of its congregation. The synagogue is an awe-inspiring structure, but the true value of Shaarey Zedek lies in neither its soaring facade nor in its brilliant stained glass, but rather in its members, those committed to its faith, the community of families who, with the care and guidance of its spiritual and lay leadership, shall surely go forth from strength to strength.

The ner tomid — the eternal lamp — burns perpetually in front of the ark as a reminder of the menorah in the Temple (Ex. 27:20; Lev. 24:2). Max M. Somberg, Neil Zechman, and Manuel Zechman hold the sanctuary lamp from the old synagogue at Willis and Brush.

The long, vibrant, creative history of Congregation Shaarey Zedek is testimony to the continuing link of one generation to another; we are indeed blessed as we see the children of our members who, upon adulthood and marriage, add their names to the membership roster of Shaarey Zedek. By American standards, our congregation is aged and venerable, but this is a synagogue that is young in spirit because of those who renew its strength.

A man spoke to me recently about what it was like for his father to belong to Shaarey Zedek in the 1930s, in the years of the Depression. The family budget had to be watched very carefully to provide for the necessities of life, and it was a struggle to pay what today we would consider a very nominal sum for membership. And this young man said that his father explained to the family that belonging to a synagogue, identifying with its heritage and sharing in its fellowship, was worth the sacrifice and had supreme value in his life. That kind of devotion, expressed by word and deed, was etched on the consciousness of a second generation and served as a powerful motivation for their desire to identify with the synagogue.

We use the word "tradition" as if it were something identified with the whole body of Jewish law and lore, something that can be placed objectively on view in the cases of a museum. But tradition is a living entity, a way of living and looking at the world which one generation hands on to the next, and its quality is dependent on those who live it. The qualities of the spirit that have sustained the Jewish tradition have been handed from one generation to the next. What was transmitted first was a continuity of faith, because when a Jew joins a synagogue, he performs a religious act. He makes a covenant which is at the very center of Jewish existence. We began our career as a people thousands of years ago at Sinai with a collective vow to assume sacred tasks, to be unique and apart, and to fulfill a sacred dream. That covenant, once made, was renewed by each successive generation. Those who belong to a synagogue renew, in the ways of their time, the ancient vow and the age-old pledge, to be a "kingdom of priests and a holy nation."

The individual member of our synagogue has not been a faceless, anonymous follower, passive, unconcerned, and detached, but has endowed this institution with warmth and devotion. Each has participated in services and recited words of prayer and expressed his support in times of difficulty. Shaarey Zedek members have not wavered in their faithfulness to the synagogue, and their loyalty remains now, as it has ever been, one of our most precious resources.

In preserving our remembrance of the past, we strengthen our faith in the promise of the future. We believe that we can provide a Jewish upbringing for our children and that the Jewish tradition will find renewal in our lives and in the lives of those whom we guide. We hope that our homes will express the sanctity which will preserve the strength of the family, and we hope that the land of Israel will be secure, that the Jewish people will be brought closer to redemption, that all mankind will know peace and justice. By our continuing identification with the synagogue, we affirm the faith that these ideals, preserved for us, will be realized for all the generations to follow.

Zechor yemoth olam, "Remember the days of old, consider the years of each generation." Thus did Moses, in his song of farewell, command the chidren of Israel. *Olam* ("eternal, everlasting") can refer to history, both past and future, as well as to people; in Jewish tradition, history, eternity, and people are one. And as we celebrate our 120 years as a Jewish congregation in an American metropolis, we also celebrate the continuity of Jewish faith, in which the past is everlasting and the people eternal.

Rabbi Irwin Groner
In part from the Sabbath sermon of June 14, 1975

Appendix

			Rabbis
Rabbi M. Sapper	1861-1863		
Rabbi A. Shappera	1863-1865		
Rabbi Laser Kontrovitch	1865-1867		
Rabbi A. Goldsmith	1867-1870		
Rabbi B. Moskowitz	1870-1877		
Rabbi E. Rosenzweig	1877-1881		
Rabbi Joseph Rappaport	1881-1883		
Rabbi Louis Bloomgarden	1883-1884		
Rabbi M. Caplan	1884-1889		
Rabbi Aaron M. Ashinsky	1889-1896		
Rabbi H. L. Cohen	1896-1897		
Rabbi Judah L. Levin	1897-1904		
Rabbi Rudolph Farber	1904-1907		
Rabbi Abraham M. Hershman	1907-1946		
	1946-1959	rabbi emeritus	
Rabbi Morris Adler	1938-1941	assistant rabbi	
	1941-1946	associate rabbi	
	1946-1966	rabbi	
Rabbi Irwin Groner	1959-1967	assistant rabbi	
	1967-	rabbi	

		Assistant Rabbis
Rabbi Gershon Rosenstock	1945-1946	
Rabbi Benjamin H. Gorrelick	1949-1950	
Rabbi Milton Arm	1954-1958	
Rabbi Gerald A. Teller	1967-1970	
Rabbi Howard V. Lifshitz	1973-1976	
Rabbi Alan B. Lucas	1978-1981	

Cantors	Cantor Chaim Wasserczuck Winchell	
	Cantor Moses Rogoff	1902-1908
	Cantor Moses Zornitsky	1908-1910
	Cantor Moses Dlugoff	1910-1915
	Cantor Abraham Minkowski	1915-1924
	Cantor Samuel Vigoda	1924-1927
	Cantor Elias Zaludkowski	1927-1932
	Cantor Jacob H. Sonenklar	1932-1969
		1969- cantor emeritus
	Cantor Jacob Barkin	1969-1978
	Cantor Chaim Najman	1979-
Associate Cantors	Cantor Reuven Frankel	1956-1967; 1969-1970
	Cantor Sidney Rube	1966-

Staff

Joseph Abrahams	1947-1955	**Executive Directors**
Wilbur S. Stein	1956-1961	
Howard S. Danzig	1961-1972	
Leo Chak	1972-1975	
Dennis Rice	1975-1980	
Thomas Jablonski	1981-	

Meyer Smith	1890-1915	**Sextons**
Hirsh B. Alper	1920-1940	
Jacob A. Epel	1940-1972	

Charlotte Shapiro	1957-1980	**Administrative Assistant**

Eliot S. Schwartz	1950-1955	**Education Directors**
Dr. Eli Grad	1956-1965	
Dr. Joshua Weinstein	1966-1969	
Howard Fishman, School Principal	1969-1970	
Rabbi Gerald A. Teller	1970-1979	
Itzhak Tatelbaum, School Principal	1979-1980	
Albert E. Karbal, School Principal	1980-1981	
Marvin Kasoff	1981-	

Jessica Zimmerman	1956-1968	**Beth Hayeled Directors**
Rosaline Gilson	1968-	

Synagogue Presidents

Hiram Kraushaar   1862-1866; 1867-1868
Harris Solomon   1866-1867
Morris Mendelsohn   1868-1870
Reuben Mendelsohn ⎫
Aaron Simon   ⎬   1876-1889
Louis Blumberg ⎭
Alexander Tannenholz   1889-1903

Manuel Herzberg
1870-1876

Samuel N. Ginsburg
1876-1878

William Saulson
1903-1908

David W. Simons
1908-1920

Joseph Wetsman
1920-1922

Louis Granet
1922-1923

Harry B. Keidan
1923-1924

Maurice H. Zackheim
1924; 1936-1939

Abraham Srere
1925-1926

Robert Marwil
1926-1929

A. Louis Gordon
1929-1932

Isaac Shetzer
1932-1936; 1939-1941

Morris H. Blumberg
1941-1944

Harry Cohen
1944-1947

Harry B. Shulman
1947-1950

Charles Rubiner
1950-1953

Leonard Sidlow
1953-1956

Hyman Safran
1956-1958

Louis Berry
1958-1959; 1965-1967

Abraham Satovsky
1959-1962

David M. Miro
1962-1965

Samuel C. Kovan
1967-1969

Samuel Krohn
1969-1971

Max L. Lichter
1971-1973

Robert A. Steinberg
1973-1975

Harold Berry
1975-1977

William M. Davidson
1977-1979

Leonard E. Baron
1979-1981

Harvey L. Weisberg
1981-

161

Sisterhood Presidents

Laura Simons	1906-1907
Gussie Herstein	1907-1909
Fanny Dembowsky	1909-1911
Millie Kaufman	1911-1913
Sarah Kaplan	1913-1920
Mary Zemon	1920-1923
Julia Zechman	1923-1925
Rebecca Zackheim	1925-1927
Lillian Smith	1928-1931
Florence Warner	1931-1933
Belle Lichtig	1933-1934
Rebecca Zackheim	1934-1938
Ethel Robinson	1938-1940
Lena Silberblatt	1940-1941
Lillian Smith	1942-1944
Sadie Spevakow	1944-1946
Bea Katzman	1946-1949
Vivian (Tatken) Berry	1949-1952
Belle Shugarman	1952-1955
Fayga Keidan	1955-1958
Elsie Deutch	1958-1960
Esther Benson	1960-1963
Rose Meskin	1963-1965
Tillie Martin	1965-1968
Sharon Fleischman	1968-1970
Diane Shekter	1970-1973
Rhea Brody	1973-1975
Betsy Bayer	1975-1977
Cynthia Steinberg	1977-1979
Marjorie Saulson	1979-1981
Joyce Blum	1981-

Men's Club Presidents

Simon Shetzer	
Hyman A. Keidan	Committee of Founders
Theodore Levin	
Jay Israel Jay	1919-1920
Arthur S. Purdy	1920-1924; 1932-1934
Harry M. Shulman	1934-1936
Elconan Saulson	1936-1938
Maurice Seligman	1938-1939; 1943-1946
Joseph Radner	1939-1941
Martin Cowan	1941-1942
Norman N. Snyder	1942-1943
Morris M. Burstein	1946-1947
Albert Green	1947-1948
Abraham Satovsky	1948-1951
Samuel J. Burke	1951-1952
Carl S. Schiller	1952-1954
Edward Robinson	1954-1955
Max L. Lichter	1955-1957
Abe Katzman	1957-1959
I. Murray Jacobs	1959-1961
George C. Parzen	1961-1963
Davis A. Benson	1963-1965
Leonard E. Baron	1965-1967
David A. Goldman	1967-1968
Bernard Breyer	1968-1970
Myron L. Milgrom	1970-1972
Marvin Fleischman	1972-1974
Jerry G. Margolis	1974-1976
Irving Laker	1976-1978
Bertrand Jacobs	1978-1980
Leonard P. Baruch	1980-

Young Married League Presidents

William A. Yolles	1953-1955
Hubert J. Sidlow	1955-1957
S. Lawrence Aronsson	1957-1959
Leonard E. Baron	1959-1961
Robert A. Steinberg	1961-1963
Eliot Charlip	1963-1965
Seth H. Barsky	1965-1967
Ira Jaffe	1967-1969
Burton H. Schwartz	1969-1971
Joel Serlin	1971-1973
Stuart Goldstein	1973-1974
Neill B. Klein	1974-1975
Paul J. Lefkowitz	1975-1976

Chairmen of the Board of Trustees
Clover Hill Park Cemetery

David W. Simons	1919-1927
David S. Zemon	1927-1943
Louis Stoll	1943-1949
Seymour J. Frank	1949-1957
Milton M. Maddin	1957-1962
Samuel Rubiner	1962-1970
Leonard Sidlow	1970-1975
Louis Berry	1975-1978
Mandell L. Berman	1978-

Chevra Kadisha Presidents
Congregation Shaarey Zedek
Established July, 1919

Joseph Ehrlich	
Isaac Saulson	
Isaac Shetzer	
David S. Zemon	
Meyer Stone	
Maurice H. Zackheim	
Louis Stoll	
Samuel Sternberg	c.1939-1950
Harry M. Shulman	1950-1960
Louis Tobin	1960-1966
Samuel Eder	1966-1974
Max M. Somberg	1974-1976
Joseph E. Goodstein	1976-

Harold Berry
Louis Berry
Thomas Borman
William M. Davidson
Henry Dorfman
Walter L. Field
Max. M. Fisher
Meyer M. Fishman
Nathan Fishman
Edward Fleischman
Joseph Frenkel
Irwin Green
Louis Hamburger
Samuel Hamburger
Joseph H. Jackier
Jay M. Kogan
Malcolm S. Lowenstein
Milford Nemer
Hyman Safran
Max M. Shaye
Joseph B. Slatkin
A. Alfred Taubman
Harvey L. Weisberg
Peter Weisberg

Shomrim Fellowship
Established 1976

Chaverim Fellowship
Established 1977

Marvin Aronovitz
Leonard E. Baron
Mandell L. Berman
Jerry Bielfield
Larry Blau
Louis C. Blumberg
Roger Boesky
Allen Charlupski
Maurice Cohen
Avern L. Cohn
Daniel C. Cullen
Joseph H. Deutch
Reubin Dubrinsky
Sidney I. Feldman
Arnold Feuerman
Irwin S. Field
Samuel Fishman
Marvin Fleischman
Sidney Forbes
Noel Gage
Martin R. Goldman
Joseph E. Goodstein
Samuel Grand
Rabbi Irwin Groner
Joel Hamburger
Erwin Harvith
David B. Hermelin
Irving M. Hermelin
David B. Holtzman
I. Murray Jacobs
Hannah Karbal
Michael Karbal

Ronald Karbal
Seymour Karbal
Joseph Katz
Irving Laker
Henry Lee
Seymour Lichter
Milton M. Maddin
Milton K. Mahler
Peter A. Martin
Martin Mattler
Harold A. Maxmen
Irvin Meckler
Louis Milgrom
Myron L. Milgrom
Albert Newman
Graham A. Orley
Joseph H. Orley
Harold S. Podolsky
Terry Podolsky
Tubie Resnik
Alvin B. Robinson
Hershel Sandberg
Saul S. Saulson
Morton L. Scholnick
Alvin B. Spector
Robert A. Steinberg
Joel Tauber
Harold S. Victor
Melvin Wallace
Bernard Weisberg
Lillian R. Wetsman
Michael A. Weingarden

Endowment Board
Established 1981

Cantor Jacob H. Sonenklar	1968
Past Presidents of the Congregation	1969
Goldie Adler	1970
Jacob A. Epel	1971
Irwin Green	1972
Louis Berry	1973
Clara & Peter Weisberg	1974
Tillie & Peter A. Martin	1975
Joseph H. Jackier	1976
Harold Berry	1977
Hannah Karbal	1978
Frieda & Edward Fleischman	1979
Graham A. & Joseph H. Orley	1980
Henry Dorfman	1981

Israel Bonds Honorees

1981 Synagogue Staff

Rabbi: Irwin Groner
Cantor: Chaim Najman
Associate Cantor: Sidney Rube
Executive Director: Thomas Jablonski
Education-Youth Director: Marvin Kasoff
Beth Hayeled Director: Rosaline Gilson

Learning Resource Center Director: Albert E. Karbal
High School Administrator: Jonathon Fishbane

Seated (left to right): Cantor Sidney Rube,
Rabbi Irwin Groner, Rosaline Gilson; *standing
(left to right):* Thomas Jablonski, Cantor
Chaim Najman, Marvin Kasoff.

120th Anniversary Committee

Goldie Adler
James M. August
Nita Barak
Leonard E. & Nancy Baron
Leonard P. Baruch
Esther Benson
Mandell L. Berman
Barbara & Harold Berry
Louis Berry
Joyce Blum
Rhea Brody
Judith Cantor
Ilene Chait
William M. Davidson
Elsie Deutch
Michael S. Feldman
Walter L. Field
Sharon Fleischman
Perry Goldman
Harold W. Goodman
Henry Green
Irwin Green
Miriam Hamburger
Joseph H. Jackier
Shelley & Lawrence Jackier
Bertrand Jacobs
I. Murray Jacobs
Lawrence Jonas
Arleen Karbal
Bea Katzman

Walter E. Klein
Samuel C. Kovan
Yale Levin
Max L. Lichter
Rose Meskin
David M. Miro
Milford Nemer
Anne Parzen
Charles Rubiner
Celia Kliger Ruda
Hyman Safran
Abraham Satovsky
Marjorie Saulson
Rose Schiller
Max M. Shaye
Yetta Shiener
Leonard Sidlow
Carmi M. Slomovitz
Robert A. Steinberg
Dorothy Wagner
Melvin Wallace
Harvey L. Weisberg
Melba Winer

Ex-Officio
Rabbi Irwin Groner
Thomas Jablonski
Marvin Kasoff
Cantor Chaim Najman
Charlotte Shapiro

Bertha Aaron
Samuel S. & Lillian Aaron
Stanley & Carole Aaron
Alan T. Ackerman
Franklin Z. & Sharon Adell
Marvin M. & Betty Adell
Joel S. & Judith Adelman
Dale & Deborah Adelson
Norman & Anne Adilman
Goldie Adler
A. Arnold & Marilyn Agree
Charles N. & Sara Agree
Samuel & Dorothy Albert
Ruth L. Allender
Gertrude Alpern
Peter M. & Ellen Alter
Jules & Deborah Altman
William & Ruth Appel
William C. Jr. & Sharon Appel
David A. Appelman
Gerald Appelman
Howard B. & Rhea Appelman
Eugene & Marcia Applebaum
Harry & Linda Applebaum
Max & Esther Applebaum
Ida Arfa
Marvin & Adria Aronovitz
Harry B. & Roslyn Aronow
Dora Aronsson
S. Lawrence & Dolores Aronsson
David & Hinda Askenazy
Samuel & Ann Atlin
Harry E. & Helen August
Herman A. and Evelyn August
James M. & Doris August
Henry Auslander
Irving & Sophie Auslander
Fred & Deanna Averbuch
Gilbert & Sophie Averbuch
Sidney & Elizabeth Averbuch
Herman & May Axelrod

Sam & Ilene Babcock
Benjamin H. & Ida Bader
Eugene & Elaine Baker
Ida Baker
Harry & Rebecca Balberor
Michael & Deborah Balkin
Firooz & Rana Banooni
Saeed & Parvane Banooni
George Barahal
Max M. & Reva Barahal
Eddy & Dorothy Barak
Morton & Nita Barak
David & Etta Barbas
Joseph & Shirley Barenholtz
Sylvia Barnett
Leonard E. & Nancy Baron
Leo & Lanie Baron
Marion Baron
Gerald & Frances Barsky
Harry C. & Lillian Barsky
Seth H. & Donna Barsky
Leonard P. & Ann Baruch
Sidney & Geraldine Baskin
Arthur & Selma Bassoff
Carl & Betsy Bayer
Robert B. & Margaret Bayer
Harvey & Phyllis Beaver
Fannie Becher
Sidney & Sharlene Beck
Sherman & Rosalind Becker
Morris & Marcia Bednarsh
Charles & Arlene Beerman
Philip & Lois Begun
Elliot I. & Molly Beitner
Norman H. & Ruth Beitner
Alan M. & Elaine Belkin
Jack W. & Linda Belkin
Maurice & Harriette Belkin
Golda Benavie
Lawrence & Beverly Benderoff
Samuel M. & Hattie Benderoff
Earl & Beverly Bennett
Davis A. & Esther Benson
Ronald & Linda Benson
Eli & Shulamith Benstein
Bruce Beresh
Clifford & Ruth Beresh
Harry Beresh

Louis & Vivian Beresh
Howard P. & Margaret Berger
Ann Berke
Evelyn Berke
Michael & Sharon Berkovic
Harry Berkowitz
Fannie Berman
Esther Berman
Mandell L. & Madeleine Berman
Marvin & Marilou Berman
Seymour D. & Rose Berman
David M. & Karen Bernard
David & Pearl Bernstein
Gerson & Lee Bernstein
Hazel Bernstein
Morris & Sylvia Bernstein
Ralph Bernstein
Rose Bernstein
Samuel I. & Susan Bernstein
Ronald & Deborah Berris
Annette Berry
Harold & Barbara Berry
Lawrence A. & Sharon Berry
Louis & Vivian Berry
Milton L. & Vivian Berry
Robert L. & Carmen Biederman
Harvey & Nathalie Bielfield
Jerry & Eileen Bielfield
Leonard & Marlene Bieman
Jerrold M. & Lynn Bigelman
Helen Biller
Sanford H. & Susan Birnholtz
Tony & Linda Blanchfield
Larry & Diane Blau
Jerry & Ilene Blaz
Frederick & Doris Blechman
Isaak & Sonia Blechman
Richard D. & Phyllis Bleznak
Ivan S. & Linda Bloch
Alan J. & Elaine Block
Belle Bloom
Phyllis Bloomberg
George L. & Joyce Blum
Bettye Blumberg
Louis C. Blumberg
Max & Ruth Blumberg
Ruth Blumberg
Hattie Blumenau

Judith Blumeno
Harold & Penny Blumenstein
George & Mae Blumenthal
Albert & Belena Boesky
Norman & Sheila Bolton
Luba Bond
Stuart & Patricia Bordman
Leonard & Lillyan Borin
Jeffrey Borin
Ralph & Phyllis Borin
Thomas A. & Sara Borin
Claudia Borin-Bock
Nathan A. & Annette Borinstein
Leonard S. & Roberta Borman
Paul & Marlene Borman
Paul D. Borman
Rose Borman
Thomas & Sarah Borman
Nathan & Mollie Borofsky
Floyd & Esther Bornstein
Frederic J. & Teri Bornstein
Lois Bornstein
Ruth Bornstein
Gerald C. & Eileen Borsand
Eugene & Joan Bortnick
Benjamin & Frances Boxman
Donald & Marcia Boxman
David L. & Debra Boyer
Stanley & Sandra Boykansky
Leonard & Ann Brand
Sidney & Anne Brand
Joseph H. & Esther Brandt
Sam & Helen Braverman
Freddie & Roberta Breitberg
George K. & Elsie Bremen
Robert L. & Harriet Brent
Bernard A. & Mildred Breyer
Michael M. & Melody Breyer
Murray & Elaine Brickman
Barry L. & Cheryl Brickner
Sidney I. & Rachel Brickner
Harold & Irma Brode
Henry & Dorothy Brode
Herbert A. & Joan Brode
Leonard & Helen Brode
Seymour & Dolores Brode
Celia Broder
Jeffrey C. & Sue Ellen Broder

Bernard & Ruthan Brodsky
Anna Brody
Benjamin F. & Carolyn Brody
Lee B. & Theodosia Brody
Robert D. & Rhea Brody
Stephen A. & Carol Bromberg
Barney & Minnie Broner
David & Lily Broner
Esther Bronstein
Selma Brookstein
Bernard & Dolly Brown
John L. Brown
Peter & Dorothy Brown
Richard M. & Sharon Brown
Rochelle Brown
Rose Brown
William J. & Edna Brown
Gertrude Bruss
Joel & Lauren Bruss
Rose Buchalter
Lee Buckman
Helen Budman
Louise Budman
Benjamin & Mary Burdick
Albert & Estelle Burke
Irving & Dorothy Burke
Perry & Ruth Burnstine
Albert & Florence Burrows
Harry & Ann Burstein
Jean Burstein
I. Marvin Burstein
Richard J. & Gayle Burstein
Richard & Elaine Burton

Joseph & Ruth Cabot
Abraham C. & Suzan Cannon
Bernard J. & Judith Cantor
Mildred Cantor
Robert M. & Rhoda Cantor
Charles M. & Marci Canvasser
Anne Caplan
Donna Caplan
Ethel Caplan
Henry & Jean Carnick
Belden & Natalie Carroll
Carl & Ann Carron
Paul & Marion Cavaler
Nellie Chad
Louis H. & Ida Chaenko
David J. & Ilene Chait
Eliot & Sheila Charlip
Florence Charlip
Sylvia Charlip
Allen & Franka Charlupski
Morey & Millie Charmer
Bessie Chase
Sheldon H. & Madlyn Chatlin
Harvey & Adela Chayet
Howard & Judith Chazen
Herbert & Frances Chernick
Viola Chernick
Marvin & Helene Cherrin
Michael J. & Sandra Cherrin
Ben S. & Lillian Chinitz
Murray & Joan Chodak
George & Valerie Chodoroff
Mandel & Toby Chudnow
Sol & Celia Cicurel
James T. & Yona Clarke
Stephen J. & Carol Coden
Pearl Coffman
Pauline Coggan
Samuel & Esther Coggan
Irene Cohan
Alan D. & Rhona Cohen
Alberto & Bertha Cohen
Arnold & Phyllis Cohen
Clara Cohen
Edward Cohen
Esther Cohen
Fred H. & Frances Cohen
Ida Cohen

Jerome A. & Rena Cohen
John & Robin Cohen
Lawrence & Shirley Cohen
Maurice & Margo Cohen
Perry & Margo Cohen
Philip & Bertha Cohen
Ronald S. & Linda Cohen
Sophia Cohen
Avern L. & Joyce Cohn
Lilly Cohn
Norman A. & Charlene Colbert
Sherwood & Sharron Colburn
Walter & Judith Coleman
David & Reba Colman
Wallace & Cynthia Colvin
Milton S. & Elaine Conway
Simon L. & Sandra Cook
Annette Cooper
Harold Cooper
Meyer I. & Fannie Cooper
Rose Cooper
Tillie Cott
Harvey & Edith Covensky
Donald L. & Helen Coville
Benjamin E. & Rose Cowan
Gladys Croll
Leo J. & Elizabeth Croll
Daniel C. & Sayde Cullen
Ben & Arlene Cutler
Helen Cutler
Maynard L. & Rita Cutler
David A. & Susan Cuttner

Christine Dabrowski
Benjamin & Gladys Daitch
Harold J. & Cynthia Daitch
Marvin C. & Peggy Daitch
Naomi Dallen
Loren S. & Sharon Daniels
Moe & Dorothy Dann
Howard Danzig
Trudy Danzig
Esther Davidoff
Belle Davidson
Sarah Davidson
Tillie Davidson
William M. Davidson
Benjamin S. & Carolyn Davis
Lewis D. & Miriam Davis
George A. & Vivian Dean
Sarah Deitch
David L. & Joanne Denn
Harvey A. & Lenore Deutch
Irwin J. & Elaine Deutch
Joseph H. & Elsie Deutch
Martin Deutch
Nettie Deutch
James L. & Cathy Deutchman
Irving & Helen Diem
Mark L. & Marilyn Diem
Sidney & Rose Diem
Philip A. & Dorothy Diskin
Charles & Rosalie Disner
Simon & Sara Dolin
Jules & Ann Doneson
Eliezer & Jenny Dorfman
Henry & Mala Dorfman
Hiram A. & Lucille Dorfman
Benjamin W. & Edith Dovitz
Esther D. Dresser
Belle Dubrinsky
Gerald H. & Phyllis Dubrinsky
Irving Dubrinsky
Marvin & Ellen Dubrinsky
Reubin & Yetta Dubrinsky
Rose Dubrinsky
Seymour N. & Carol Dubrinsky
Ethel Dunitz
Sarah Dunn
Mel L. & Renee Durbin
Albert H. & Bertha Dworkin
Jean Ruth Dyblie

S. Robert & Doris Easton
Lawrence & Audrey Edelheit
Bernard Edelman
Bessie Edelman
Morris & Ruth Edelman
Ivan T. & Sandra Edelstein
Renee Edelstein
Naomi Eder
Milton & Elaine Einstandig
Newton & Sybil Einstandig
Philip Einstandig
Gary A. & Barbara Eisenberg
Florence Eisenberg
Lawrence & Barbara Eisenberg
Gerald M. & Carole Eisenshtadt
Bernard & Phyllis Eisenstein
David & Evelyn Eisman
Jeffrey & Nancy Eisman
Maxwell H. & Anne Elgot
Nathan Elkus
Philip L. & Estelle Elkus
Elmer P. & Peggy Ellias
Frank J. & Lisa Ellias
Harold & Betty Ellias
William & Sheila Ellman
Israel & Paula Elpern
Sarah Elson
Isaac & Judy Engelbaum
Ethel Epel
Joseph & Beatrice Epel
Robert & Florence Eppstein
Earle I. & Beth Erman
Jack & Hilda Erman

Fred & Mary Faber
David & Ida Falik
Ira E. & Bella Falk
David I. & Sally Fand
S. Joseph & Lilo Fauman
Joel J. Faust
Ruth Faust
Norman W. & Helen Feder
Gustave & Ruth Feig
Rose Feigenson
Minnie Fein
Charles & Lenore Feinberg
George & Selma Feinberg
Paul C. & Shirley Feinberg
Pearl Feinberg
Anne Feldman
Henry & Manya Feldman
Joseph D. & Sally Feldman
Michael & Debra Feldman
Michael S. & Marcy Feldman
Mitchell & Helen Feldman
Oscar H. & Barbara Feldman
Robert & Sharon Feldman
Sidney I. & Beth Feldman
Joel H. & Laura Feldmesser
Albert & Edith Feldstein
Joseph Feldstein
Betty Fenley
Arnold & Thelma Feuerman
Irwin S. & Joanna Field
Walter L. & Lea Field
Irene Fierberg
Jerome & Joanne Finck
Fred & Gisele Findling
Morris I. & Pauline Fine
Clarissa Fineman
Rebecca Fineman
Sharon Fineman
Joseph & Shirley Finkel
Marvin & Shirley Finkel
Edwin G. & Blanche Finsilver
Howard H. & Devorah Finsilver
Lloyd M. & Frances Finsilver
Rose Finsilver
Stuart & Iris Finsilver
Morey H. & Nettie Firestone
Nathan & Ardell Firestone
Arthur J. & Patricia Fischer

Joseph M. & Marsha Fischer
Jonathan & Beth Fishbane
Betty Fisher
Gordon & Lois Fisher
Max M. & Marjorie Fisher
Shirley Fisher
Alvin M. & Mary Lee Fishman
Benjamin & Shirley Fishman
Betty Fishman
David B. & Deena Fishman
Ellis & Geraldine Fishman
Gordon & Hanna Fishman
Lloyd E. & Estelle Fishman
Meyer M. Fishman
Milton & Dolores Fishman
Milton N. & Rita Fishman
Morris R. & Ethel Fishman
Nathan & Sarah Fishman
Samuel & Sarah Fishman
Sidney & Bertha Fishman
Irving J. & Gloria Flanders
Barry M. & Karen Fleischer
Arthur & Roberta Fleischman
Edward & Frieda Fleischman
Marvin & Sharon Fleischman
Maurice & Naomi Floch
Elliot B. & Rita Folbe
Sidney & Madeline Forbes
Sidney & Henrietta Foreman
Philip J. & Sadye Forman
Sol D. & Hilda Forman
Dave & Lois Foster
Donald & Nancy Fox
David & Beverly Frank
Edith Frank
Harvey & Esther Frank
Robert G. & Bryna Frank
Seymour J. & Ethel Frank
Rose Frankel
Roman & Elayne Franklin
Douglas & Dorothy Frazein
John & Hazel Frazer
Charles Fredman
Jack & Mary Freedland
Bob & Marilyn Freedman
David & Sadie Freedman
Jeanne L. Freedman
Michael W. & Edith Freeman

Andrew A. & Eva Freier
Joseph Frenkel
Marvin & Barbara Frenkel
Jennie B. Fried
Louis & Virginia Fried
Ruth Friedberg
Jack Friedlander
Abba I. & Allison Friedman
Alfred & Francine Friedman
Bernard A. & Lillian Friedman
David I. & Phyllis Friedman
Eli & Ethelene Friedman
Florence Friedman
Harry P. & Beverly Friedman
Leon & Minnie Friedman
Marilyn L. Friedman
Morton & Deborah Friedman
Ralph & Mildred Friedman
Richard & Audrie Friedman
Sanford & Harriet Friedman
Stanley B. & Miriam Friedman
Murray & Bess Frumin
Owen H. & Rita Frumin
Helen Fuller

Noel & Hilda Gage
Gary E. & Barbara Galens
Gilbert J. & Jane Galens
Esther P. Galin
Gary S. & Gina Galin
Louis I. & Becky Galin
Robert M. & Elayne Galin
Ellis I. & Olga Gans
Robert I. & Sue Gans
Abram Gardin
Joel F. & Linda Garfield
Bernice Garon
Sydney E. & Susan Gartenberg
Arnold & Diane Gartner
Louis R. & Rose Gelfand
Rose Geltner
Eugene A. & Reinart Gelzayd
Sarah Gendelman
Tillie Gendil
Martin & Sharon Gene
Samuel Gerendasy
Morton S. Gerenraich
Tillie Germansky
Byron H. & Dorothy Gerson
Alice Gilbert
Allan W. & Anita Gilbert
Daniel H. & Jo Gilbert
Edith Gilbert
Joseph G. & Shyrle Gilbert
Milton R. & Dawn Gilman
Russel & Rosaline Gilson
Jack Ginsburg
May Ginsburg
Ida Gladstone
Alex & Rosalyn Glanz
Samuel & Lillian Glanz
Ilene Berris Glaser
Lillian Glass
Louis & Paula Glazier
Sidney & Ellen Glen
Maurice L. & Sarah Glicklin
Steven H. & Brenda Glickman
Edward D. & Francine Gold
Irving P. Gold
Louis Gold
Miriam Gold
Paul M. & Linda Gold
Ruben & Lillian Gold

David & Florence Goldberg
Jack & Harriet Goldberg
Mark J. & Miriam Goldberg
Milford & Beatrice Golden
Sally Golden
Murray & Linda Goldenberg
Aubrey & Shirley Goldman
David A. & Harriett Goldman
Dorothy Goldman
Irving & Belle Goldman
Martin B. & Linda Goldman
Morris & Carol Goldman
Perry & Sybil Goldman
Samuel & Edith Goldman
Samuel R. & Bette Goldman
Seymour B. Goldman
Sheldon A. & Rose Goldman
Sidney H. & Barbara Goldman
Herbert L. & Barbara Goldstein
Lawrence & Barbara Goldstein
Lillian M. Goldstein
Maxwell & Sylvia Goldstein
Meyer L. Goldstein
Samuel L. & Ruthe Goldstein
Stuart & Iris Goldstein
Michael H. & Carol Golob
Mettie Golub
Henry & Arlene Gonte
Roy S. Good
Conrad & Florence Goode
Jack J. & Sylvia Goode
Martin & Elaine Goode
Arthur L. & Charlotte Goodman
Charles M. & Sylvia Goodman
Charlotte Goodman
Harold W. & Evelyn Goodman
Michael & Francine Goodman
Nettie Goodman
Philip & Julia Goodman
Sam H. & Ruth Goodman
Walter A. & Geraldine Goodman
Walter Alan & Harriet Goodman
William M. & Sandra Goodman
Joseph E. & Helen Goodstein
Stuart & Gail Goodstein
Herbert H. & Barbara Goodwin
Anna Gordon
Belle Gordon

Benjamin B. & Gertrude Gordon
Harvey A. & Clara Gordon
Louis & Eleanor Gordon
Mary Gordon
Milton M. & Sheryl Gordon
Norman & Rhea Gordon
Rhea Gordon
Ruth Gordon (Mrs. Milton)
Ruth Gordon
Seymour & Marilynn Gordon
Seymour V. & Maryum Gordon
Fred & Eleanor Goren
Gerald & Jean Goren
Herman & Jean Goren
Irwin & Donna Goren
Louis & Leona Gothelf
Clarence & Adelina Gottesman
Milton & Sylvia Gottesman
Benjamin Gould
Paul S. & Arline Gould
Louis A. & Ida Goutman
Frances Grand
Samuel & Evelyn Grand
Belva Granet
Ralph & Geraldine Granet
Arnold S. & Barbara Grant
Barry M. & Elizabeth Grant
Abe & Rose Green
Fanya Green
Felix & Betty Green
Howard L. & Bettie Green
Henry & Edna Green
Henry L. & Loretta Green
Irwin & Bethea Green
Jack & Dorothy Green
Marvin S. & Shirley Green
Rose Green
Sam & Anne Green
Wesley S. & Arlene Green
Jerome B. & Judith Greenbaum
Ida Greenberg
Jack L. & Rose Greenberg
John L. & Bernice Greenberg
Julius J. & Evelyn Greenberg
Marsha A. Greenberg
Robert S. & Eileen Greenberger
Allen F. & Joan Greenfield
Esther B. Greenhouse

Belle Greenwald
Irwin & Leypsa Groner
Jerome & Marlene Gropman
Emery & Roberta Grosinger
Norma Grosinger
Arnold S. & Paula Gross
Morris & Toba Gross
Leo Grossman
David M. Gubow
Estelle Gubow
Joel L. & Phyllis Gurstell
Lawrence E. & Sharon Gurstein
Ben & Sara Gurvitz
Robert C. & June Gurwin
Benjamin R. & Ruth Gutow
Jack Guz
Judith Guz

Louis & Sonia Haas
Donald & Natalie Hadesman
Joel & Hilda Hamburger
Louis & Ethel Hamburger
Robert L. & Merrill Hamburger
Samuel & Miriam Hamburger
Ettie Handelman
Gertrude Handler
Wallace M. & Marlene Handler
Gerald H. & Madeline Harris
Nathan Harris
Richard A. & Cynthia Harte
Alan J. & Freda Harvith
Erwin & Sylvia Harvith
Samuel G. & Rosella Harvith
Alan J. & Anita Hayman
Stephen P. & Linda Hayman
Louis E. & Ethel Heideman
Bessie Helper
Gary N. Helper
Harold & Beatrice Helper
Adelaide Helpert
Sidney Helpert
Leon J. & Anna Herman
David B. & Doreen Hermelin
Irving M. & Florence Hermelin
Benjamin & Haya Hershkovitz
Louis F. & Eleanor Heyman
Mary Heyman
Sidney J. & Florence Hillenberg
Mason & Anna Himelhoch
Reuben & Bess Himelstein
Harold Hirshman
Fannie Hochman
Leon & Sharon Hochman
Morton M. & Dorothy Hochman
Sheldon & Laena Hoenig
Allan M. & Rochelle Hoff
Myles B. & Marsha Hoffert
Harold & Virginia Hoffman
Maxwell M. & Leah Hoffman
David B. & Deanna Holtzman
Irwin T. & Shirley Holtzman
Paul & Carol Hooberman
Alan E. & Lori Horowitz
Michael & Barbara Horowitz
Steven C. & Robin Horowitz
Harvey R. & Marilyn Hortick

Victor S. & Sally Horvitz
Audree Horwitz
Marvin Q. & Gail Horwitz
Harry & Harriet Housman
Norma T. Hudosh
Moris & Rose Huppert
Samuel & Sylvia Hurvitz

Samuel & Valerie Indenbaum
Paul & Roberta Ingber
Theodore & Sara Isaacs
Harold E. & Elaine Isaacson
Elaine Isberg
Robert D. & Berta Isgut
Harold Israel
Louis & Sarah Iwrey
Sol & Sylvia Iwrey

Thomas & Renee Jablonski
Joseph H. & Edythe Jackier
Lawrence & Rochelle Jackier
George S. & Mary Jackson
Harriet Jackson
Philip & Joyce Jackson
Betty Jacob
Esther Jacob
Martin S. & Violet Jacob
Bertrand & Muriel Jacobs
I. Murray & Sonia Jacobs
Morris M. & Caroline Jacobs
Paul A. & Lori Jacobs
Richard & Elyse Jacobs
Sidney R. & Joan Jacobs
Ira & Brenda Jaffe
Ceil Jonas
Lawrence & Shirley Jonas
Ben & Esther Jones
Myron H. & Ida Joyrich

William & Pauline Kadushin
Theresa Kahle
Douglas H. & Denise Kahn
Irwin L. & Ruth Kahn
Murray M. & Mollie Kahn
Saul B. & Felicia Kalbfeld
Belle Kamin
Helen Kanat
Irvin O. Kanat
Gerald A. Kanter
Marilyn Kanter
Philip L. Kanter
Sheldon M. & Marian Kantor
Henry S. & Mary Lili Kaplan
Howard & Ellen Kaplan
Isaac & Rachel Kaplan
John S. & Marion Kaplan
Seymour & Gertrude Kaplan
Robert D. & Lois Kaplow
Garry & Viola Kappy
Abraham & Leah Kar
Albert E. & Judy Karbal
Betty Karbal
Hannah Karbal
Michael & Arleen Karbal
Ronald & Marilyn Karbal
Seymour & Rosemarie Karbal
David & Julia Karp
Martin & Deborah Karp
Pearl Kasle
Robert & Evelyn Kasle
Barney J. & Pauline Kasoff
Marvin & Barbara Kasoff
Sol & Sarah Katser
Aaron B. & Edna Katz.
Charles & Lillian Katz
Gerald & Janice Katz
Irving Katz
Joseph & Ann Katz
Norman D. & Ann Katz
Philip S. & Barbara Katz
Samuel Katz
Samuel & Sharon Katz
Sidney F. & Sally Katz
Uri & Nili Katz
William R. & Barbara Katz
Herbert J. & Ruth Katzen
Maxwell E. & Ruth Katzen

Aaron & Gertrude Katzman
Abe & Bea Katzman
Ben L. & Marion Katzman
Harold L. & Janice Katzman
Sidney & Rhoda Katzman
Beverly Kaufman
David I. Kaufman
Harold & Dorothy Kaufman
Ira & Rose Kaufman
Jack & Sheryl Kaufman
Jerome S. & Suzanne Kaufman
Myron & Elaine Kaufman
William & Mary Kaufman
William H. & Carole Kaufman
Irving S. & Roberta Kay
Herman & Dorothy Kazdan
Louis L. & Alta Kazdan
Irving F. & Johanna Keene
Bruce H. & Carol Keidan
Fred H. & Sarah Keidan
Herbert S. & Barbara Keidan
Jacob L. & Miriam Keidan
Kate Keidan
Arthur B. & Linda Kellert
Barry & Janice Kelman
Sol & Betty Kemp
Irving D. & Bernice Kernis
Nicholas Z. & Jeny Kerin
Charles H. & Arlene Keys
John & Anne Keystone
Jerome M. & Rita Keywell
Sol & Jennie King
David H. & Ellen Kirsch
Jacob & Sheila Kirsch
Morris Klaus
Edythe Klein
Joseph & Evelyn Klein
Louis & Gladys Klein
Louis T. & Marion Klein
Maurice & Ruth Klein
Neill B. & Debrah Klein
Walter E. & Esther Klein
Shimon & Drora Kleinplatz
Lonna R. Kletter
Seymour E. & Joyce Kliger
Alfred & Ruth Klunover
Calvin & Cassandra Klyman
Maurice M. & Tillie Knopper

Sidney D. & Isabelle Kobernick
Earl R. & Helene Koenig
Erna Koenigsberg
Ronald & Jane Koenigsberg
Jay M. & Reva Kogan
Jessie Kohlenberg
Arnold & Sharyanne Kollin
Max J. & Esther Kolovsky
William & Miriam Konstantin
Frank S. & Jennie Koppelman
Eleanor Korn
Erwin & Bess Kornwise
Ann L. Korson-Berger
Bernard & Sylvia Koss
Dennis J. & Mildred Kovan
Samuel C. & Dorothy Kovan
Thomas & Barbara Kovan
Rose Koven
Mirian Kozlow
Allen & Dianna Kraft
Harry & Irene Kraft
Philip G. & Barbara Kraft
Robert F. & Joanne Kraft
Bernard & Edith Krakauer
Allen B. & Ida Kramer
Billie Kramer
Goldie Kramer
Harold A. & Sarah Kramer
Hyman A. & Bernice Kramer
Jennie Kramer
Michael & Zina Kramer
Oscar M. & Inge Kramer
Manus & Barbara Krasman
George & Selma Kratchman
D. Michael & Cynthia Kratchman
Betty Kraus
Jerome W. & Reva Krause
Josephine Krell
Raymond L. Krell
Seymour & Margery Krevsky
Bernard & Perle Kriger
Margaret Kriger
Dorothy Kripke
Jennie Krugel
Lawrence & Carol Krugel
Leonard & Michelle Krugel
Richard & Sally Krugel
Michael P. & Faye Krut

Eli H. & Reva Kuhel
Belle Kukes
Thomas & Rosanne Kukes
Freda Kurland
Ruben & Bernice Kurnetz
Maurice I. & Marjorie Kurzmann
Lillian Kuschinski
Alvin & Ruth Kushner
Sander A. & Elinor Kushner
Harold A. & Phyliss Kusnetz
Julian & Lesley Kutinsky
Morris Kutinsky
Ann Kutzen

Ben & Gloria Labe
James E. & Ellen Labes
Marvin & Alice Labes
David & Barbara Lachar
Philip E. & Adeline Lachman
Gertrude Lachover
Al & Gertrude Lahr
Gerald & Elaine Laker
Irving & Beverly Laker
Joseph J. & Sylvia Lambert
Alfred & Delphine Landau
Ann Landau
Graham & Alene Landau
Lena Lang
Joseph H. & Frieda Langnas
Aubrey M. & Tirzah Lansky
Harold & Ethel Lansky
Morris A. & Tillie Lantor
Charles & Mollie Lapides
Irwin I. & Fanny Lappin
Sheldon G. & Barbara Larky
Jacob & Estelle Lasser
Marshall D. & Carole Lasser
Martin & Helen Lattin
Carl & Jain Lauter
Miriam Lawrence
Herbert & Reva Lazarus
Saul M. & Rosalee Leach
David & Gloria Leader
Hannah Leader
David & Elaine Lebenbom
Max M. & Marian Lebowitz
Henry P. & Linda Lee
Scott & Susan Leemaster
Fannie Lefkofsky
Julian & Ruth Lefkowitz
Paul J. & Janice Lefkowitz
Betty Lehrman
Alden M. & Lorraine Leib
Burton H. & Victoria Leib
Joel K. & Barbara Leib
Sidney Z. & Marion Leib
Sam & Gloria Lerman
A. Martin & Helen Lerner
Leonard H. & Lorraine Lerner
Selma Lerner
J. Philip & Ethel Levant
Julian & Deborah Levant

Cyril C. & Lois Levenson
Janet Levenson
Joel & Lynn Levi
Ruth Levi
Arleene G. Levin
Charles L. & Patricia Levin
Morris & Bonnie Levin
Murray B. & Shirley Levin
Ralph & Edith Levin
Rhoda Levin
Ruth Levin
Sima Levin
Sylvia Levin
William & Belle Levin
Yale & Anna Levin
David & Evelyn Levine
Harold A. & Lee Levine
Jerold M. & Lynne Levine
Joseph & Edith Levine
Max & Edythe Levine
Saul & Stella Le Vine
Seymour J. & Lois Levine
Donald H. & Sadie Levinson
S. Daniel & Geri Levit
Charlotte Levitan
Jack & Sandra Levitt
Burton T. & Francine Levy
Charles M. & Marilyn Levy
Jerome B. & Marise Levy
Robert A. & Helen Levy
A. Bart & Susan Lewis
Donald & Leah Lewis
Ida Lewis
Alvin B. & Shirley Lezell
Richard L. & Susan Lezell
Arthur & Vivian Libby
Adolph H. & Rose Lichter
Max L. & Buena Lichter
Seymour & Betty Lichter
Belle Lichtig
Frederick & Naomi Lichtman
Libbie Lieberman
Gertrude Lieberoff
Katherine Liebschutz
Herman M. & Pola Lifton
Bernard & Lauretta Limond
Ada Linden
Melvin D. & Rene Linden

Zedek, by Morris Brose.

Ben P. & Winifred Lindenbaum
Sander & Randee Lipman
Carl E. & Lorelei Lipnik
Jacqueline Lipshaw
Rebecca Lipshaw
Rose Lipsitz
David T. & Edith Lipton
Jeffrey I. & Sharon Lipton
Raymond F. & Claire Lipton
Steven L. & Eva Lipton
Bernard & Bettina Lis
Ann Loewenberg
Bernard & Sherry Lofman

Edmund L. & Suzanne London
Leon & Annette London
Seymour S. & Evelyn Lowen
Beth Lowenstein
Daniel D. & Helene Lublin
Sheldon B. & Phyllis Lublin
Benjamin & Ann Luborsky
Ruth Luckoff
Joel A. & Barbara Lutz
Sheldon M. & Gail Lutz
Sherwin & Annette Lutz
Sidney & Diane Chambers Lutz
Irving M. & Sarah Lyons

Milton & Esther Maddin
Michael W. & Donna Maddin
Jennie Madorsky
Samuel J. & Pamela Magar
Irving C. & Sarah Mahler
Milton K. & Bertha Mahler
David B. & Ellen Maiseloff
Ruth Malerman
Anne Mall
Ben D. & Sadie Maltzman
Jerald B. & Carole Maltzman
Leslie & Sarah Mandel
Morris J. Mandell
Seymour N. & Pearl Manello
Rose Manning
Anne Marans
Michael B. Marcus
Daniel R. & Linda Marcus
David & Arlene Margolin
Jerry G. & Geraldine Margolis
Peter A. & Sharon Martin
Kenneth W. & Judith Matasar
Minnie Matler
Raye Matler
Gloria Matthews
Martin & Elaine Mattler
Sheldon I. & Dolores Max
Harold A. & Ethel Maxmen
Irvin & Lillian Meckler
Abram & Rhoda Medow
Irving A. & Lillian Meisner
Ivan I. & Ruth Meisner
Robert M. & Joan Meisner
Philip & Carol Meizels
Carol Melinn
Gerald & Irene Mellin
Esther Mendelsohn
Esther Mendelson
Irving & Judith Mendelson
Morrie & Rachel Mendelson
Julius S. & Rose Meskin
Russell E. & Annette Meskin
Morton & Carol Metzger
Agusta Meyers
Bruce M. & Phyllis Meyers
Charles & Miriam Meyers
Ronald M. & Rena Meyers
Samuel C. & Lillian Meyers

Berta Meyerson
William H. & Sheri Michaels
Arnold S. & Florence Michlin
Norman & Bernice Michlin
Bernard & Callista Mikol
Charles & Florence Milan
Samuel & Laura Milan
Bruce C. & Rita Milen
Jack W. & Dorothy Milen
Louis & Thelma Milgrom
Myron L. & Jacqueline Milgrom
Beatrice Miller
George J. & Charlotte Miller
Herman & Jean Miller
Martin & Beverly Miller
Milton M. & Rose Miller
Norman S. & Paula Miller
Philip & Karolyn Miller
Ralph & Ruth Miller
Neil S. & Anita Millman
Nathan L. & Rose Milstein
David M. & Bernice Miro
Edward & Shelly Mishal
Beverly Mitchell
Marian Mittenthal
Stuart R. Mittenthal
Mollie Moers
George & Irma Mogill
David S. & Leslie Molitz
Arnold & Charlotte Monash
Adele Mondry
Mayer & Sheila Morganroth
David H. Morrison
Nathalie Morrison
Stephan R. & Barbara Morse
Lillian L. Mosen
Donald & Lynda Moses
Ken & Carolyn Moses
Charles L. & Miriam Moss
Edwin & Belle Moss
Norman D. & Ann Moss
Ben & Tillie Mossman
Douglas & Linda Mossman
Sol & Ruth Myers

Chaim & Sherry Najman
Julia Nathan
Hyman & Bessie Nathan
Milton L. & Sandra Nathanson
Corinne Nayer
Philip & Blanche Needle
Harry L. & Lois Nelson
Milford & Ilene Nemer
Morris & Anna Nemer
Leroy S. & Brenda Neumann
Albert & Phyllis Newman
Fredric M. & Marsha Newman
Eva Newman
Gus D. Newman
Joseph H. & Eleanor Newman
Robert C. & Jacqueline Newman
Rudolph J. & Ann Newman
Alan & Judith Nickamin
Charles & Nancy Nida
Solomon M. & Aliza Nivy
Richard & Marcia Nodel
Harold & Evelyn Noveck
Donald A. & Gertrude Nusholtz
Robert & Susan Nusholtz
Walter S. & Diana Nussbaum

Sam M. & Gertrude Oistacher
Sam & Frieda Olen
Philip & Rae Olender
Theodore & Lillian Olender
Jules B. & Barbara Olsman
Henry S. & Judy Orbach
Leo D. & Sheila Ordin
Geoffrey A. & Klara Orley
George & Isabel Orley
Graham A. & Sally Orley
Joseph H. & Suzanne Orley
Alexander & Harriet Ornstein
Herman & Helen Osnos
Claude & Terry Oster
Philip & Marlene Ozrovitz

Stuart M. & Gertrude Palmer
Daniel & Sandra Panush
Sol & Sylvia Panush
Louis & Tillie Panush
Harry B. & Eleanor Park
Elliott M. & Denise Parr
Louis & Gail Parr
George C. & Anne Parzen
Steven J. & Susan Parzen
Betty Passman
Benjamin & Evelyn Paxton
Allan & Donna Pearlman
Frederic M. Pearlman
Gail Pearlman
Marvin B. & Rhoda Perlin
Charles & Elaine Perlman
Jack W. & Lillian Perlman
Michael B. & Diane Perlman
Stuart L. & Elaine Perlman
Edward & Frances Perlmuter
Allen L. & Mildred Pick
Sally Pick
Ralph & Adrian Pierce
Albert J. & Adeline Pines
Marcus & Lillian Plotkin
Arnold M. & Lynn Podolsky
Harold M. & Ruth Podolsky
Harold S. & Shirley Podolsky
Seymour E. & Dorothy Podolsky
Terry & Meryl Podolsky
Joseph Pohl
David & Elaine Polk
Sidney E. & Esther Pollick
Sal & Sonia Pone
Herbert & Janet Pont
Bernard N. & Christine Portnoy
Lawrence & Jaclyn Portnoy
Nathan B. & Sarah Portnoy
Robert G. & Maida Portnoy
Sarah Portnoy
Helen Posner
Norman & Susan Prady
Milton L. & Fae Prag
Milford R. Pregerson
Beatrice Prenzlauer
Florence Primack
Jack Prinstein
Jack & Rose Provizer

Harold & Joan Provizer
Antoinette Purdy
Donald J. Purther
Douglas & Shirley Purther
Franklin & Sonia Purther

Bert & Helene Rabinowitz
Bernice Radner
Celia R. Radner
Edward L. & Susan Radner
Irving & Belle Radner
Abner I. & Alice Ragins
Irving Raimi
Jacob & Sylvia Raimi
Leonard R. & Celia Raimi
Lawrence & Jo Raizman
Janet Randolph
Steven & Judith Rapp
Richard & Frances Rassler
Benjamin & Rosalyn Reder
Charles J. & Sally Reich
Samuel & Barbara Reider
Maurice B. & Ruth Reistman
Albert & Lois Resnick
Barry & Elaine Resnick
Gertrude Resnik
Ida Reznick
Samuel J. & Arlene Rhodes
Fannie Rice
Harry L. & Lillian Rice
Marvin & Judith Rich
Ellis B. & Rita Rifkin
Frederic A. & Gloria Rivkin
Ida S. Robbins
David M. & Marjorie Roberts
Saul & Virginia Robins
Alvin B. & Fannie Robinson
Belle Robinson
Bud & Phyllis Robinson
David & Lois Robinson
Eli E. & Zelda Robinson
Jack & Aviva Robinson
Jay H. & Barbara Robinson
Rose Robinson
Steven & Rhonda Robinson
Warren & Davida Doneson Robinson
Louis P. & Rosalind Rochkind

Gary & Ilene Rochlen
Albert & Sophia Roggin
Irving & Ida Rogovein
Markus & Mona Rohtbart
Irving & Marilyn Rollinger
Robert & Susan Rollinger
Norman & Helen Rom
Aaron & Rose Rose
Dora Rose
Joseph B. Rose
Paul & Marian Rose
Tilly Rose
Gerald & Estelle Rosen
Leonard J. & Sharon Rosen
Rachel Rosen
Frank & Joyce Rosenbaum
Baruch & Sonia Rosenberg
Mildred B. Rosenberg
Oscar & Gloria Rosenberg
Sara Rosenberg
Charles & Isabelle Rosenblatt
Stanley P. & Marilyn Rosenfeld
Frieda Rosenshine
Benjamin F. & Maria Rosenthal
Esther Rosenthal
Irwin E. & Anne Rosenthal
Jay M. & Dorothy Rosenthal
L. Hudson & Edith Rosenthal
Lawrence M. & Abby Rosenthal
Sylvia Rosenthal
Eveline Ross
William & Gail Rossen
Herbert W. & Sandra Rossin
Anna Roth
Michael A. & Linda Roth
Harry & Rose Rott
Sheldon & Carol Rott
Leon & Adeline Rottenberg
Shirley Rottman
Sidney & Esther Rube
Sharon Ruben
Erwin A. & Judith Rubenstein
Jack & Rose Rubin
Max & Alene Rubin
Elsie Rubin
Arthur J. & Sally Rubiner
Charles & Sylvia Rubiner
Dorothy Rubiner

William & Marcia Rubinoff
David & Barbara Rubinstein
Mark & Andrea Rubinstein
Richard A. & Elizabeth Rubinstein
Margie Ruby
Louis & Celia Ruda
Edith Rudner
Theodore & Evelyn Rudner
Morris & Elizabeth Ruskin
Philip & Alice Ruskin
Robert & Beth Ruskin
Paul L. & Harriett Ruza
Edward & Shirley Ruzumna

Benjamin J. & Lottie Sabin
Mitchell E. & Marilynn Sabin
Nison & Doreen Sabin
Kolmon Z. & Pearl Sachse
Benjamin J. & Ethel Safir
David & Elizabeth Safran
Fred D. & Anne Safran
Hyman & Leah Safran
James A. & Diane Safran
Kenneth J. & Barbara Safran
Mark B. & Peggy Saffer
Leonard & Linda Sahn
Ann Sake
Joseph & Rita Salama
Arthur O. & Bette Salasnek
Harold K. Salasnek
Lowell M. & Beverly Salasnek
Rita Salasnek
Arthur W. & Florence Saltzman
Clarence & Harriet Salzberg
Max Salzberg
Rose Samelson
Gladys Sampson
Wally & Rochelle Sampson
Fred & Miriam Samson
Alex & Ida Samuels
Hershel & Lois Sandberg
Ethel Sandelman
Eugene N. & Sylvia Sands
Henry & Gail Sandweiss
Shaindel Sandweiss
Sheldon & Miriam Sandweiss
Charles Sarasohn
Alan B. & Gwen Sarko
Sam & Lillian Sarver
Moe & Tania Saslove
Abraham & Toby Satovsky
Lester & Margarette Satovsky
Mildred Satovsky
Neil A. & Jean Satovsky
Sheldon B. & Sharon Satovsky
Stanley L. & Phyllis Satovsky
Fannie W. Saulson
Herman J. & Helen Saulson
Manton N. & Betty Saulson
Saul S. & Marjorie Saulson
William W. Saulson
Beulah Sauter

Joseph F. & Diane Savin
Stella Savin
Lawrence B. & Hannah Schanes
Joel P. & Ellen Schaumberg
Julius & Rose Schaumberg
Ethel Schatz
Emma Schaver
Daniel E. & Sandra Schechter
Hyman Schechter
Julius & Hilda Schechter
Martha Schechter
Neal & Marilyn Schechter
Robert & Bluma Schechter
Dennis H. & Judith Scheinfield
Edwin J. & Marilyn Schiff
Judith Schiff
Lawrence Schiff
Robert A. & Ann Schiff
Anne Schiller
Estelle Schiller
Donald & Maxine Schiller
Maurice S. & Marjory Schiller
Richard & Laura Schiller
Robert & Jane Schiller
Rose Schiller
Myrna Schlafer
Richard M. & Ilene Schlaff
Bernard D. & Ann Schlussel
Edward I. & Lillian Schlussel
Hershel & Toby Schlussel
Lawrence A. Schlussel
Murray & Rosanne Schlussel
Abe A. & Doris Schmier
Herbert & Faye Schnaar
Edwin C. & Maryon Schneider
Jerold I. & Lesley Schneider
Paul & Phyllis Schneider
Jack & Ruth Schneyer
Morton L. & Diane Scholnick
Nathan H. & Beatrice Scholnick
Michael Schor
Hanley & Joan Schreiber
Harold Z. & Susan Schreiber
Elliot I. & Lorraine Schubiner
Elliot C. Schubiner
Dorothy Schubiner
David L. & Thelma Schurgin
Alan S. & Sandra Schwartz

Anne Schwartz
Barney J. & Rhea Schwartz
Betty Schwartz
Burton H. & Mary Schwartz
David Schwartz
Gail Schwartz
Gilbert F. & Phyllis Schwartz
Jeanette Schwartz
Mary Schwartz
Melvin Schwartz & Synde Keywell
Richard & Marlene Schwartz
Robert H. & Linda Schwartz
Samuel S. & Mae Schwartz
Sara Schwartz
Benjamin & Shirley Schwimmer
Andrew E. & Alice Segal
David S. & Roberta Segel
Manuel & Ethel Segel
Burton M. Seidon
Jennie Seiton
Stephen & Maureen Selfon
Steven B. & Bonnie Seligson
Bruce E. & Suretta Selik
Maurice E. & Rose Sell
Howard A. & Nancy Serlin
Louis & Anne Serlin
Max & Ida Serlin
Seymour & Annette Serling
Jeffrey S. & Linda Serman
William & Elaine Serman
Jeffrey P. & Donna Serwin
Morris & Sylvia Serwin
George D. & Florence Seyburn
Jerold W. & Shirley Shagrin
Charlotte Shapiro
Donald Shapiro
Frances Shapiro
Jack & Miriam Shapiro
Hilda Shapiro
Leonard & Ethel Shapiro
Milton Shapiro
Seymour & Ethel Shapiro
Susan Shapiro
Bruce L. & Joan Shatanoff
Paul H. & Freda Shawn
Max M. & Dorothy Shaye
Leo & Carol Sheiner
Rose Sheinfeld

Joseph & Lilyan Shekter
Murray A. & Diane Shekter
Sabra Shekter
Sam A. & Margie Shell
Edward & Esther Sherman
Gerald & Renee Sherman
Ruth Sherman
Gloria Shetzer
Samuel & Lama Shetzer
Alfred S. & Shirley Shevin
Joseph & Ann Shewach
Michael B. & Linda Shewach
Phillip & Yetta Shiener
Victor & Alfrieda Shiffman
Louis & Bellien Shiovitz
Albert & Dorothy Shipko
Leo & Roslyn Shipko
Dorothy Shlain
Frances Shufro
Joseph & Evelyn Shulman
Florence Shuman
Nathan E. & Sarah Shur
Thelma Shwedel
Marvin S. & Dorie Shwedel
Franklin D. & Harriet Siden
Minette Sidlow
Hubert J. & Clarice Sidlow
Leonard & Leonore Sidlow
Byron E. & Bobette Siegel
Charles J. & Esther Siegel
Daniel & Blanche Siegel
George H. & Lenore Siegel
Marvin D. & Gloria Siegel
Peter Siegel
Rosalind Siegel
Robert L. & Rhoda Siegel
Robert W. & Joyce Siegel
Julius & Ceil Sigman
Dora Silets
Arthur & Rhoda Sills
Allen B. & Nancy Silvarman
Joseph M. & Rhea Silver
Michael S. & Bari Silver
Emma Silverman
Esther Silverman
Gilbert B. & Lila Silverman
Isadore & Evelyn Silverman
Julius S. & Helen Silverman

Mollie Silverman
Morris I. & Shayna Silverman
Ruth Silverman
Mildred Silverstein
William R. & Charlotte Silverstone
Mitchell & Carolyn Simmer
Annette Simon
Irving & Dorothy Simon
Michael F. & Naida Simon
Max E. & Mildred Simon
Ruth Simon
Sheldon & Ethel Simons
Alex & Mildred Sklar
David & Connie Sklar
Leo P. & Libby Sklar
Manuel & Harriet Sklar
Norma Sklar
Ray & Carolyn Skop
David L. & Mollie Sky
Goldie Slakter
Abe & Joyce Slaim
Joseph B. & Edith Slatkin
Martin & Linda Slepian
Carmi M. & Sharron Slomovitz
Philip & Anna Slomovitz
Irwin A. & Susan Small
Richard A. & Leanne Small
Morton D. & Harriett Smerling
Abraham J. & Rose Smith
Donald A. & Carol Smith
Lillian Smith (Mrs. Charles A.)
Lillian Smith (Mrs. Raymond)
Marion Smith
Roslyn Smith
Sue Smith
Toba Smokler
Arthur & June Snider
Charles & Leah Snider
Harvey G. & Selma Snider
Joseph C. & Edith Snider
Norman M. & Edith Snider
Reuben & Margaret Snider
Simeon Snider
Norman N. & Judith Snyder
Wolf & Esther Snyder
Howard B. & Ann Sobel
Samuel R. & Carole Sobel
Jack & Eleanor Sol

Gary & Carol Sole
Sion & Elaine Soleymani
Jack & Jane Solomon
Jerome H. & Diane Solomon
Sam & Rae Solomon
Terese Solomon
Max M. & Belle Somberg
Jacob H. Sonenklar
Jerome & Adele Sonenklar
Sol & Hilda Sonenklar
Martin & Betty Sorkowitz
Louis D. & Marilyn Soverinsky
Allan & Irene Sparage
Ida Spear
Alvin B. & Lois Spector
Bertram J. & Audrey Spiwak
Fanny Srere
Meyer & Rose Stamell
Morton & Perle Stahl
Morris & Betty Starkman
Gerald M. & Gail Starler
Maurice Starr
Jerome S. & Betty Stasson
Albert H. Stein
Esther Stein
Harvey & Alice Stein
Leonard & June Stein
S. Lawrence & Marion Stein
Belle Steinberg
Esther Steinberg
Jonathan J. & Susan Steinberg
Robert A. & Cynthia Steinberg
David & Ethel Steinman
Pearl Stellar
Fay Stern
Harold H. & Vera Stern
Joel & Norman Stern
Milton & Barbara Stern
William & Judy Stern
Samuel & Carolin Sternberg
Vernon & Merle Sternhill
Rose Stewart
Lawrence & Beverly Stillwater
Louis J. & Ruth Stober
Sid Stober
Reva Taubman Stocker
Robert D. & Andrea Stoler
Dora Stoll

Stuart R. & Elisa Stoller
Bernard H. & Barbara Stollman
Ethel Stollman
Sidney & Jean Stolsky
Alan J. & Lee Stone
Grace M. Stone
Howard & Beverly Stone
Miriam Stone
Sheldon R. & Donna Stone
Sidney L. & Betty Stone
Alan Stotsky
Rudolph J. & Betty Straus
Max P. & Selma Stromer
Merrill B. & Ruth Stromer
Isadore Strub
Samuel & Judith Stulberg
Helen Sucher
A. Albert & Beatrice Sugar
H. Saul & Wilma Sugar
Maurice D. & Phyllis Sugar
Marcus H. & Eleanore Sugarman
Samuel & Judy Sugerman

Harry D. & Jeannie Tabor
Robert & Elizabeth Tam
Norman G. & Ferah Tarockoff
Joel Tauber
Shelby Tauber
A. Alfred Taubman
Aaron & Jennie Taylor
Lillian Teitelbaum
Bennett S. Terebelo
Max & Sylvia Thomas
Marshall & Rhoda Tobin
Michael E. & Susan Tobin
Morton L. & Diana Tobin
Zilpah Tobin
Bernard L. & Marlene Toft
Harry & Lucy Topcik
Larry R. & Toby Trager
Charles L. & Sandra Traugott
Steven L. & Barbara Tronstein
Allen & Ronda Tuchklaper
Floyd S. & Gail Tukel
Irving & Barbara Tukel
Sam & Rose Tukel
Sherwin & Emily Tukel
Ethel Tyner

Gertrude Ungar
Alex & Faye Ullmann
Gerald & Frances Uzansky

Anna Rose Vass
Harold S. & Marjorie Victor
Howard J. & Gail Victor
Janet Victor
Jennie Victor
Lyle D. Victor
Norberto Voloschin

Donald & Dorothy Wagner
Ronald J. & Ava Wagner
Samuel & Ida Wagner
Molly Wainger
Steven & Diana Wainess
Martin & Debra Waldman
Saul & Sylvia Waldman
David & Barbara Wallace
Elaine Wallace
Fay Wallace
Melvin & Helene Wallace
Samuel M. & Enid Wapner
Shirley Warner
Allan & Elizabeth Warnick
Anne Warren
Seymour & Doris Wasserman
Lewis C. & Rae Wassermann
Meyer & Rose Waterstone
Elaine Wax
Harvey Wax
Reuben D. & Rena Wax
Seymour & Ruth Wayne
Herbert N. & Harriet Waze
Sidney H. & Ann Weber
Louis Wechsler
Philip & Wilma Wechsler
Marvin S. & Joyce Weckstein
Martin & Lorraine Wedgle
Helen Wein
Henrietta Weinberg
Joseph & Lea Weinberg
Max & June Weinberg
Nettie Weinberg
Rae Weinberg
Sydney & Connie Weinberg
Ernest J. & Barbara Weiner
Gershon R. & Jean Weiner
Leo & Betty Weiner
Earl & Shirley Weingarden
George & Libby Weingarden
Michael A. & Linda Weingarden
Samuel & Peggy Weingarden
Sidney Weingarden
Terry L. & Susan Weingarden
Joel Weingarten
Morris Weingarten
Nettie Weingarten
Leonard A. & Jane Weinstein

Mae Weintraub
Murray & Barbara Weintraub
Ronald & Rena Weintraub
Alvin A. & Henrietta Weisberg
Beatrice Weisberg
Bernard & Helen Weisberg
Harold I. & Marion Weisberg
Itzhak & Ruchi Weisberg
Harry Weisberg
Harvey L. & Lucille Weisberg
Peter & Clara Weisberg
Joseph & Faye Weisblatt
Celia Weisman
Kate Weisman
Arthur J. & Gayle Weiss
Lillian Weiss
Morris & Sandra Weiss
Robert & Audrey Weiss
George & Ida Weiswasser
Philip & Eve Weltman
Manya Weston
Harry Wetsman
Lillian R. Wetsman
William & Muriel Wetsman
William M. & Janis Wetsman
Lanee Wexler
Joel E. & Susan White
Rosetta Whitefield
Leon A. Wiener
Albert A. & Maurine Williams
Richard D. & Marian Williams
Michael F. & Nomi Wilenkin
Sara Wilenkin
Sidney J. & Melba Winer
Beryl Winkelman
Eric & Barbara Winkelman
Iliene Winkelman
Sheldon P. & Rissa Winkelman
Harold L. & Mildred Winston
Edward & Evelyn Wishnetsky
Lawrence & Eileen Wittenberg
Stephen & Sandra Wittenberg
Gladys K. Witus
Kenneth & Sharon Wolf
Charles S. & Carol Wolfe
Sara Wolk
Rose Wolrauch

Alma Derin Yaffe
Samuel & Fay Yagoda
Morton I. & Ruth Yarrows
Max Yorke
WIlliam A. & Shirley Yolles
Irving & Leah Yura

David P. & Evelyn Zack
Samuel N. & Gloria Zack
Harvey B. & Linda Zalla
Lois Zamler
Bess Zechman
Dorothy Zechman
A. Robert Zeff
Lester Zeff
Meyer B. & Grace Zeff
Michael & Jane Zeid
Samuel & Sarah Zeldes
Edward & Lillian Zellman
Robert & Magdalene Zeman
Sol & Molly Zeme
Ethel Zieger
Henry L. & Stephanie Ziff
Emanuel R. & Sylvia Zingeser
Richard & Shirley Zirkin
Laura Zolkower
Mollie Zolkower
Leonard S. Zubroff
Leonard & Marsha Zucker
Alex & Anne Zuckman
Morris Zuckman
Saul & Blanche Zuieback
Miriam Zussman

Family Chronicle

Family Chronicle

Husband _____

Birth Date _____

Wife _____

Birth Date _____

_____

Married _____

clergy _____

at _____

_____

Children _____

_____

_____

_____

_____

Grandchildren _____

_____

_____

_____

_____

_____

_____

_____

_____

_____

Generations Affiliated with
Congregation Shaarey Zedek

Parents _____

_____

_____

_____

Grandparents _____

_____

_____

_____

_____

_____

Others _____

_____

_____

_____

_____

_____

_____

_____

_____

_____

_____

Family Chronicle

Husband's Family

_____   _____
Father   Mother

_____   _____   _____   _____
Father   Mother   Father   Mother

_____   _____   _____   _____   _____   _____   _____   _____
Father   Mother   Father   Mother   Father   Mother   Father   Mother

Wife's Family

_____   _____
Father   Mother

_____   _____   _____   _____
Father   Mother   Father   Mother

_____   _____   _____   _____   _____   _____   _____   _____
Father   Mother   Father   Mother   Father   Mother   Father   Mother

Family Chronicle

Simchas. Occasion, date, place

_____

_____

_____

_____

_____

_____

_____

Yahrzeit Record. Name, date of death, place of interment

_____

_____

_____

_____

_____

_____

_____

_____

_____